GW00537672

THE LAST ANZACS

Lest We Forget

THE LAST ANZACS

Lest We Forget

TEXT
TONY STEPHENS

PHOTOGRAPHS
STEVEN SIEWERT

Fremantle Arts Centre Press

Australia's finest small publisher

At last the order came, and we moved off down the beach, crowded now with the waiting wounded. Some were smiling and smoking, some had agony on their faces, and some there were whose faces I could not see. 'Shall we be like this soon?', we thought. Over the first rise from the sea we went into the hell of shrapnel. Men started to fall amongst us now. We halted under cover of a dry watercourse, and there we left our packs. Up through the valley we went again, men still falling, and bullets whistling past … we met more wounded men being helped and carried along. Some of them urged us on, though their silent wounds were enough for that. 'Give it to them for us, boys,' one of them said. 'They can't fight like us …'

Harley Mathews, at Gallipoli, 1915

Christ at Gallipoli

This synod is convinced that the forces of the Allies are being used of God
to vindicate the rights of the weak and to maintain the moral order of the world.

Anglican Synod, Melbourne, 1916

Bit weird at first,
That starey look in the eyes,
The hair down past his shoulders,
But after a go with the ship's barber,
A sea-water shower and the old slouch hat
Across his ears, he started to look the part.
Took him a while to get the way
A bayonet fits the old Lee-Enfield,
But going in on the boats
He looked calmer than any of us,
Just gazing in over the swell
Where the cliffs looked black against the sky.
When we hit he fairly raced in through the waves,
Then up the beach, swerving like a full-back at the end
When the Turks'd really got on to us.
Time we all caught up,
He was off like a flash, up the cliffs,
After his first machine gun.
He'd done for three Turks when we got there,
The fourth was a gibbering mess.
Seeing him wave that blood-red bayonet,
I reckoned we were glad
To have him on the side.

Geoff Page

Contents

Acknowledgements

Thanks are due, above all, to the Anzacs, for their patience and good cheer. We are indebted to the families and friends who helped with the interviews, the photographic sessions and the provision of material. We also thank the copyright holders of the published poems and editors of the *Sydney Morning Herald*, who provided time and resources and originally published some of these words and photographs. We are grateful, too, to the Australian War Memorial, the Australian Department of Veterans' Affairs, the New Zealand Returned Services' Association, Sir Roden Cutler for his foreword and Dr Michael McKernan for his written contribution and for checking the other words.

Tony Stephens

ANZAC: Then and Now

Military Road, Mosman, Sydney, is a busy place at any time but it is hectic around Christmas. With prosperity abundant, Christmas 1995, in the eigtieth anniversary year of Gallipoli, found the antique shops, specialist food retailers, and boutiques full of all sorts of shoppers and, predominantly, it was a young crowd. There is a consistency of building style among these shops; most of them are Federation style buildings, some untouched, others beautifully renovated and restored. One stands out — the Country Road store, an outlet for smart casual clothes and homewares. A two-storey building of imposing proportions, with a grand entrance, high ceilings and original fittings, the shop also boasts a foundation stone set by the former Governor-General, Lord Forster. The shopper, if more inquisitive than acquisitive, will discover that this store was, in an earlier existence, Mosman's Anzac Memorial Hall.

Built with funds provided by public subscription, the hall was intended as a home away from home for members of the Mosman sub-branch of the Returned Sailors', Soldiers' and Airmen's Imperial League of Australia, the major veterans' group in Australia established during World War I. The hall was designed to provide office and meeting space for members of the league, a billiards room and other recreational facilities, and lockers for members in which they might store their beer. Mosman being Mosman, the hall would not be given a liquor licence.[1]

The foundation stones for the 'memorial clubhouse', as it was first described, were laid at a ceremony held two days before Anzac Day 1921, that is, in the sixth anniversary year. Among those to witness the impressively solemn ceremony was Mosman's member of Federal Parliament, General Sir Granville Ryrie, who was also the Assistant Minister for Defence. 'A downright Tory', Ryrie mixed easily with all sections of the community, and had a reputation for blunt, forceful speaking. Twice wounded at Gallipoli, and fighting in the desert with the Anzac Mounted Division, Ryrie in command stood up for his men and won widespread affection.[2] He would have been warmly welcomed by the returned soldiers as he made his way to the official enclosure at Mosman in 1921. There he was joined by the New South Wales president of the RSL, the Mayor of Mosman, and assorted military figures. In welcoming the Governor-General, the mayor, Alderman Dedden, claimed that 'in Mosman they did not talk loyalty — they lived it — and their brand was British-Australian'.[3] He was not to know that the house brand of later years would boast goods made in many parts of the world.

Lord Forster, appointed Governor-General in October 1920, had lost his only two sons to the war, and thus spoke with feeling about the need to 'take deep, loving and abiding interest in those who have fought and died for us'. He expected, he said, that these memorial clubrooms would help those who had served their country, and would perpetuate the memory of those who had died. He believed that the hall would preserve the spirit of comradeship, which found its origin in war. 'Such a spirit can never die,' Forster predicted, 'but institutions such as this may do much to perpetuate it and give it practical scope.'[4] The foundation stone, and the building's elaborate title built in bricks high above the entrance, are today the only reminders that this was once a special place, out of bounds to commerce, a place apart.

As the old soldiers fade away, their clubrooms fall into disrepair and disuse and may, as in Richmond, Victoria, become an up-market gymnasium for sweaty young things, or, as in Mosman, a fashionable shop. The collapse of these once cherished institutions, mocking their everlasting future that the Governor-General had predicted, warns us that with the passing of the veterans Australia's Anzac legend may also collapse and be forgotten.

When the distinguished Australian historian K.S. Inglis travelled to Gallipoli in 1965 with a party of original Anzacs for the fiftieth anniversary, he remarked on the 'infirmity' of his travelling companions. Thirty years later, remarkably, some of them were still alive, as this book testifies, but their number was few indeed. In 1965 when the old diggers landed at Anzac Cove they were greeted, as Inglis recorded, by 'about a hundred people: cameramen, reporters, war veterans, soldiers, men in suits from Istanbul, women in shawls from neighbouring villages, and four young Australian hitch-hikers, two boys and two girls, in parkas and jeans'.[5] Inglis reported that the veterans greeted the hitch-hikers with enthusiasm, seeing in their presence 'unexpected evidence that some young Australians cared about the Anzac tradition'.

In 1965 few, apparently, believed that an interest

and pride in Australia's military past could be expected of the young. And yet today Gallipoli draws thousands of young Australians to its gentle beaches and astounding gullies and hills. Gallipoli, I am told, rivals the Munich beer festival as the 'in' destination for the thousands of young Australians who roam Europe relentlessly, month after month, in search of knowledge, entertainment and fun.[6] On Anzac Day 1995 there were several thousand young Australians at the Dawn Service at Gallipoli and their disappointment when things went wrong and the service was delayed was readily apparent. When another party of veterans returned to the peninsula in 1990 for the seventy-fifth anniversary schoolchildren were turned out by their teachers all along Sydney's Pacific Highway to farewell them. On arrival at Istanbul's President Hotel the veterans were swamped by the media and by hundreds of young backpackers who confessed to great sentiment at seeing these old men in their midst. Most of these young people then made their way to Gallipoli and joined in the Dawn Service and the National Ceremony at Lone Pine with great enthusiasm. There must have been several thousand present (the newspapers reported 12,000), many of them camping on the peninsula, even in Ari Burnu cemetery, causing one Turk to remark to another: 'See how these young Australians love their heroes; they are even prepared to lie down with them.'[7]

This remarkable increase in public involvement over a thirty-year period cries out for explanation. It is matched, too, by the notable increase in attendance at Australian commemorative ceremonies on Anzac Day, or on special occasions. For Gallipoli, some would point to the much greater mobility of young Australians when comparing 1965 with 1995. In 1965 international travel was still expensive and out of the reach of many; by 1995 it was commonplace. Some would point, too, to the increased awareness of Anzac because of the impact of the popular feature film *Gallipoli*, released in Australia in 1981. Others might suggest that the extreme old age of the veterans and the media interest in them gave a sense of one last chance to the venture that aroused people's sentimental interest in a passing phase of Australia's history. Without the veterans to stimulate interest, would Gallipoli still have the same drawing power?

The well-being of history lies in its telling for unless the story is transmitted across the generations it is lost. Those who fought at Anzac shared a common history, no matter from what part of Australia they had enlisted. School teachers and school texts told them of their British heritage and drummed into them the high points of British history with William the Conqueror and Magna Carta as present to them as the story of Australian Federation. In books like *Deeds that Won the Empire* these new soldiers learnt the ways of British soldiers, and it is likely that they kept on going on that confusing day in April 1915 because of a feeling about what a British soldier would have done and a fear of being judged inferior. These men had a history of which they were proud but as they dug in at Gallipoli the astounding thought began to dawn on them that they were creating their own new nation's history. As they sat in their dugouts reading the *Bulletin* or the newspapers of their local area that family had sent them, they gained a sense of working on history's stage. A writer in *The Anzac Book* predicted a time 'when steamers will bear up the Aegean pilgrims come to do honour at the resting places of friends and kindred and to move over the charred battlegrounds of Turkey'. He was right about the volume of traffic, wrong about the mode of transport.

Today's pilgrims are not the friends of those who lie in Lone Pine Cemetery or any of the dozens of other little cemeteries that dot the peninsula. If they are related to the fallen it is a distant relationship, perhaps no stronger than the dimly remembered words of a great-grandfather recalling his lost brothers. For most who visit Gallipoli the personal or family element is lost; the drawing power is that these men were Australians, that they made history for Australia. As Prime Minister Keating said of the Unknown Australian Soldier at the ceremony of Entombment in Canberra in November 1993, 'he is one of us'.

But this sentiment alone is insufficient to ensure a continuing interest in the story of the Anzacs and in their contribution to the making of modern Australia. Listening to snatches of conversation at Anzac Cove on Anzac Day 1995 as we waited for the ceremony to begin, I began to suspect that few in the crowd could express more than a few of the most generalised ideas about the history of the place. Names like Quinn's Post or the Nek, which would bring a shudder of terror to people of my grandparents' generation, mean nothing to today's pilgrims. They need guides, of course, to make the most of their day or so at Gallipoli, but they need the story too because in modern Australia it has not been told.

There was a time when Australian military history was folk history. You only had to stand in Sydney's George Street on Anzac Day in the 1950s or 1960s to test the truth of this, for as each fresh battalion of marchers approached someone in the crowd would link the marchers with their story and their special places of honour. 'Ah, there's Jacka's Mob' someone would say or point with pride to the men who had stormed Mont St Quentin. As the years passed, however, sentiment took over and we applauded the old men for their age as much as for their deeds and we celebrated them as heroes even as we knew that we had lost the story of their heroics.

Perhaps the official histories are to blame for the failure of military history in our popular imagination for they seem unapproachable books in their size, detail, and terminology. Perhaps the way the force was organised has confused us too. It is hard to read about the 13th Battalion or the 40th and keep it in our heads; how much easier might it have been to have remembered the Hunter Valley Regiment or the City of Melbourne Light Horse, if local names had been applied to the Australian Imperial Force. We do need points of contact with our heroes, we need to have their story told and retold to us so that as Weary Dunlop stands for the prisoners on the Burma Railway, or Jacka for the bravery of Gallipoli, we can fix a few organising ideas in our minds and build knowledge around them. What we need above all is their story written in a way that allows us to understand its meaning. Like liturgy in a church, we need the story to be constantly retold on our great national days if we are to experience its meaning and pass it on. And we need a national commitment to the telling of our history in our schools, for without that the story will surely die.

There is drama enough, and mystery, too, in the landing at Anzac Cove. Standing on the heights above the beach we can imagine the horror of men landed at the wrong spot, digging into the sand to build a small barrier against the bullets from above. We can feel the shock of men seeing their mates killed, mates with whom they had lived and worked at home, with whom they had enlisted for a lark, and trained when it suited them, and travelled to places they had only dreamed about, who now lay on the beach in the ugly sprawl of death. We can hear the cries of 'stretcher-bearer' and the moans of the injured waiting for help. As the light grew brighter we can see the wild charge up the hills that rose so unexpectedly before these Anzacs, as they would soon think of themselves, and we can smile at the man who had written in his diary only a few hours earlier how coincidental it was that he was launching himself into the game of war just as the football season commenced in earnest at home. We can follow them up to the Nek and mourn the hundreds of Lighthorsemen killed in their suicidal charge that no officer had the sense or courage to call off. We can walk over the ground at Lone Pine and marvel that men fought a subterranean battle for days in the Turkish trenches, scarcely knowing whether it was night or day, or whether it was friend or foe around the next corner in the trench system. We can recall with pride that seven Australians were awarded the Victoria Cross for the fighting at Lone Pine and nod in agreement with the historian Charles Bean who claimed that so many others might easily have been similarly recognised.

Or, if we do not know their story, we can scratch our heads and wish we had known more before we made the long and difficult trip to Anzac and brighten up at the thought of the beckoning bars and bazaars of Istanbul.

Australian commemoration of our war dead has always been a matter of individuals. Look at almost any war memorial in suburban or rural Australia and you will find the list of names of those from the district who died in war and, often enough, the list of names of those who served. At the national memorial in Canberra bronze plaques along a lengthy cloister list the names of all Australian servicemen and women killed in war, the merchant navy excepted, and Australia is possibly the only nation to have attempted to list all its war dead. It was the vision of national commemoration that each life was freely offered and sacred and thus should be recorded and recalled.

In writing his histories, and in establishing the Australian tradition of official military history, Charles Bean abandoned the generals and the politicians, barely noticed the War Office in London and concentrated instead on the men at the fighting front. When a man was named in Bean's work his details were recorded too, the place and date of enlistment, his age, his work, and his fate. Through Bean we can know the Australian Imperial Force as a collection of individuals, of named and known men (and the few women admitted to their ranks as nurses), of men for whom war started as a game and grew into a desperate evil. Of men who took great pride in what they had done and who developed great love for their mates and their country in the terror of war.

This book continues the spirit of the work that Charles Bean had started because it, too, concentrates on the individuals and their life stories in telling of those few Anzacs who remain. In doing so, this book reminds us of the short span of Australian history and of the importance of that history to our national life. In knowing the men recorded in these pages we know more about Australia and what it means to be Australian. Knowing them, we mourn their passing. Those of us who love their story will want to see it told and retold to Australians over all the generations to come so that, even if the bricks and mortar of their memorials crumble or are put to other uses, the spirit, as Lord Forster had predicted, will never die.

Writing this in 1995, perhaps I was slightly too pessimistic about the continuing chances of 'Anzac Now'. Many of the trappings of the old ways of preserving Anzac in our national life were obviously falling into disuse or disrepair. The clubrooms, so central to the men of Anzac in former days, were being adapted for different purposes. Perhaps I read too much into that because churches are now also being recycled for other uses all over the country. Who has not seen for sale a delightful wooden country church, that mezzanine added, which will make a delightful home or weekend retreat? The RSL clubrooms at Captains Flat in New South Wales have similarly been turned into a somewhat draughty house. Structures can be adapted without damaging the spirit they once enshrined.

In 1995 it was possible to ponder what would be the fate of 'Anzac Now' when the last Anzac had died, but that day, we hoped, would not dawn for a while yet. But Alec Campbell, the last of them all, did die in 2002 and now we face the reality of no living contact with the story.

The response to his passing was, in any terms, extraordinary. We had come to expect a state funeral. Once reserved for the very few, prime ministers or governors-general dying in office, state funerals are more commonplace now. But this one was special and we needed to ask why it was so.

Were we prepared for the manifestations of real grief and sadness that his passing occasioned? I was in Sydney at the time of his death and everywhere officialdom was doing what it could to observe the appropriate rituals. Flags lowered on State parliament, on government buildings, beautifully, to my mind, on Anzac Bridge. But it was the response of the ordinary folk that most caught my attention. 'I feel as though

I have lost the last link with my father,' a woman friend said to me. 'He was an Anzac too, you know.' Or a card on Sydney's Cenotaph in tribute to a man personally unknown to the person placing it there. We must not exaggerate this but the grief for many was real. There was the feeling that something had gone from our lives.

As I wrote in 1995, but repeat with more emphasis now, we need, still, to tell their story to ensure that it continues to inspire the nation. But we need to tell other stories too as has been done with the renewed attention to the Kokoda Track and the epic struggle against the Japanese in 1942. I suspect that Gallipoli will continue to draw us back; for its grandeur, and for the fact that the story there was the first in line in the telling of the story of this nation in war. And for the special quality of that place. The peninsula is a place of beauty and serenity if you can get off on your own. But there is more to it than that. It speaks to you of the spirit of men who would do their best for their country and their mates; and of other men who would fight valiantly to repel this invasion. It tells, too, of the generosity of both sides in stretching out the hand of friendship to the other when the battle was over, recognising a common humanity and a shared memory of the mutual misery of their predicament.

The nation enjoyed a great privilege in knowing, in their final years, some of the very old men whose stories are told in this book. Perhaps in earlier years we had neglected them a bit but we eventually made up for that. We can pass on that sense of privilege to those coming after us who will not know them personally, as it were, by ensuring that they do know the story that should sustain our nation forever.

Michael McKernan

1   Gavin Souter, *Mosman: a History*, Melbourne 1994, p 160.
2   *Australian Dictionary of Biography*, vol 11, Melbourne 1988, pp 502–504.
3   *Sydney Morning Herald*, 25 April 1921.
4   ibid.
5   Ken Inglis, 'Gallipoli Pilgrimage 1965', *Journal of the Australian War Memorial*, no 18, April 1991, p 24.
6   Information supplied from personal enquiry by Katherine McKernan, the author's daughter.
7   *Sydney Morning Herald*, 26 April 1990; anecdote told to the author by the late Clifton Pugh who overheard the Turk's remark.

1915

Up they go, yawning,
the crack of knuckles dropped
to smooth the heaving
in their legs, while some,
ashamed, spit bile
between their teeth,
and hum to drown their stomachs.

and letters wadded thick
from Mum (who says
'always keep
some warm clothes on ...')

 Up from slits in dirt
they rise, and here they stop.
A cold long light swings over.

ANZAC: The Battlefield

And now, as he looked and saw the whole Hellespont covered with the vessels of his fleet and all the shore and every plain about Abydos as full as possible of men, Xerxes congratulated himself upon his good fortune; but after a little while he wept.

Herodotus, Book 7, Chapter 45

Australian gums grow at Gallipoli, at the Lone Pine cemetery. They have battled fierce northern winters to secure a toehold on the famous peninsula, by the hardy olives. One could make too much of the symbolism of Australian trees growing in Turkey, but Gallipoli is full of history and symbols — life and death, birth, growth, hopeful beginnings and premature endings. So the fighting gums, an Australian gift to a foreign land, have their place in the grand scheme of things.

The stones have their place, too. Try wading ashore at Anzac Cove, where the Australians and New Zealanders waded ashore in 1915, and those richly multi-coloured stones move under the invader's feet. Some Anzacs drowned here, unable to cope with their weapons, their packs, the water and, no doubt, the stones. They had travelled about 17,500 kilometres only to be denied the battle, never to fire an angry shot. The stones might have warned the Anzacs that their lives were not meant to be easy. Yet they could not have told of the hell waiting on shore.

The Anzacs had anchored in Mudros Harbour, on the island of Lemnos, opposite Troy and about one hundred kilometres from the Dardanelles. The symbols are rich here. According to legend, Agamemnon, King of Mycenae, lit a chain of fires to signal to his queen, Clytaemnestra, that he had taken Troy. Troy was the battlefield of Homeric heroes. Achilles, the greatest warrior in Agamemnon's army, killed Hector, the chief Trojan warrior, before being fatally wounded himself by Paris. Helen, the most beautiful woman in Greece, fled to Troy with Paris, thereby sparking the Trojan wars. Herodotus, the Greek author of the first great narrative history of the ancient world, wrote of Thermopylae, the narrow pass on the Greek coast, as a global conflict. He wrote of the Dardanelles, the Hellespont of ancient times, and Persian Emperor Xerxes building his bridge of boats across the Narrows in 480BC, to carry his armies for the invasion of Greece into Europe. Alexander the Great, King of Macedonia, led 20,000 men in boats 1,500 metres across the Narrows around 334BC at the beginning of the campaign that took him all the way to India. Leander is said to have swum the Narrows every night to meet Hero, the virgin priestess of Greek legend. Lord Byron swam it.

Only a few of the Australians would have been familiar with the history, the legends with a vestige of historical foundation, and the myths. A more typical Australian attitude came from Private G.S. Feist, writing from Lemnos to his mother and father in Western Australia about the frustration of waiting for orders:

'… at last the word came — we were going to have a fly at the Turks. Well you can bet it was like putting a bit of roast meat to a starving man — we sprung to it.'[1]

They sprang to it, all right. They sprang ashore just south of Ari Burnu, on a small beach about the size of Tamarama in Sydney, and wrote some history of their own. The beach was to become known within days of 25 April 1915 as Anzac Cove. The visitor cannot but be surprised by Anzak Koyu, as it's known officially in Turkey. Over the moving stones, out of the blue Aegean Sea, the invader takes about twelve paces up a beach no more than 600 metres long before being confronted by, not a gentle rise like the Anzacs had expected, but a daunting, sometimes precipitous cliff face. A naval officer shouted: 'Tell the colonel they've put us ashore in the wrong bloody place.' Yet the men laughed at adversity. 'They want to cut that shooting out,' a private complained, 'somebody might get killed.' Another said it was 'poor bloody farming country'. General Sir Ian Hamilton, the British commander watching from HMS *Queen Elizabeth*, said: 'God, one would think, cannot see them at all or He would put a stop to this sort of panorama and yet, it would be a pity if he missed it: for these fellows have been worth the making … They fight for love — all the way from the Southern Cross for love of the Old Country and of liberty.' The myths were to follow soon after.

You can see how the legend grew. Up in Walker's Ridge Cemetery is the grave of Private R.H. Robertson, 20th Battalion, Australian Infantry. He was sixteen years old when he died. 'Although his body resteth, his memory will never die,' are the words on his headstone. Down at the Anzac Cove Cemetery lie the remains of Trooper G.R. Seager. He 'died a man and closed his life's brief day ere it had scarce begun'. He was seventeen. Who could dig a grave that would not be too narrow for these boys?

Len Hall was about that age, sixteen years and five months, when he enlisted. His 10th Light Horse Regiment needed a bugler and Len could play the instrument. The recruiting officer put his age up and Len gave an emu plume from his hat to Eunice Lydiate, a girl he scarcely knew, before sailing off to war. Hall survived where Robertson and Seager could not. When he returned to Perth, Eunice Lydiate returned the plume to her hero. They were married and remained so until her death towards the end of 1995.

The human heart, then, holds the essence of war's bright hopes and sorry endings. The historians, however, must look beyond the cliffs, the gums, the stones, the callow youth and the hardened veteran. *The Oxford Companion to Australian Military History*, published in 1995, concludes the section on Gallipoli: 'As far as the Anzac troops were concerned, the only thing to be said for the Gallipoli operation was that it kept them away from the Western Front for at least a year. Had they arrived in France in early 1915 their casualty list (as operations around Pozières would subsequently prove) would certainly have been much higher than it was at Gallipoli.'[2]

This viewpoint is in stark contrast to the initial

21

On the Dead in Gallipoli

They came from safety of their own free will
To lay their young men's beauty, strong men's powers
Under the hard roots of the foreign flowers
Having beheld the Narrows from the Hill.

John Masefield

Photo: Australian War Memorial A5778

reaction to the Anzac landing, which was one of triumph. Ellis Ashmead-Bartlett, the British journalist, aroused Australian pride with his famous dispatch: 'The Australians rose to the occasion … this race of athletes proceeded to scale the cliffs.' Hamilton said they were of 'indubitably splendid fighting stuff'. John Masefield, pointing out that the Anzacs had had not more than six months' training, wrote: 'They were, however, the finest body of young men ever brought together in modern times. For physical beauty and nobility of bearing they surpassed any men I have ever seen; they walked and looked like the kings in old poems, and reminded me of the line in Shakespeare, "Baited like eagles having lately bathed". As their officers put it, "they were in the pink of condition and didn't care a damn for anybody". Most of these new and irregular formations were going into action for the first time, to receive their baptism of fire in "a feat of arms only possible to the flower of a very fine army".[3] The *Manchester Guardian* proposed in 1916 that Australia's proposed capital be called, not Canberra, but Anzac, 'the most illustrious made name in history'.[4]

The idea that Gallipoli was a defeat for the British, French, Indian, Australian and New Zealand forces has never taken hold completely. Some people argue that Australia's most celebrated people and events are failures — Ned Kelly, the Eureka Stockade, the death of explorers Burke and Wills, Gallipoli. Yet even the evacuation of Gallipoli after eight months was seen as a triumph, with some justification since the feat was achieved with only two minor injuries. When his yacht, *Australia II*, trailed three races to one in the 1983 America's Cup, Alan Bond said: 'We had our backs to the wall there [at Gallipoli] and we won that one.'[5] Professor Geoffrey Blainey says: 'In the final scoreboard Gallipoli could well be summed up by a reasonably impartial Australian umpire as an impressive draw because it was played on the enemy's home ground.'[6]

Barbara Tuchman, the distinguished American historian, says misgovernment falls into four categories: First, tyranny or oppression. Second, excessive ambition such as the challenge to England by Philip II of Spain with his Armada, Germany's twice-attempted rule of Europe by a self-conceived master race, or Japan's bid for an empire of Asia. Third, incompetence or decadence, as in the case of the Roman Empire, the last of the Romanovs and the last imperial dynasty of China. Fourth, folly or perversity. Troy — and the Trojan horse — are in the fourth category.[7] Gallipoli might qualify here, too.

Yet the folly of the invasion must be measured against its aims. With the opposing armies locked in a deadly war of attrition on the Western Front by late 1914, leaders looked for ways to break the deadlock. The Dardanelles campaign was seen as an alternative to the muddy, bloody horror of France. Knocking Turkey out of the war would open up a sea link to Russia and force Germany to face the pressure of another battlefront. Winston Churchill's refusal in 1911 to agree to a Turkish request for an alliance and his decision before Turkey joined the war to confiscate two Turkish ships might also be seen as folly. 'Scandalous, crumbling, decrepit, penniless Turkey,' said Churchill. He also called Turkey a 'stench in the nostrils of Europe'. So the Germans replaced the two ships and the Turks embraced the Germans. The misgovernment of excessive ambition was tackled by the misgovernment of folly.

The first British–French attempt to break the deadlock came with a naval attack across the Narrows in March 1915. Turkish mines and howitzers destroyed the attack and the Turks look upon the

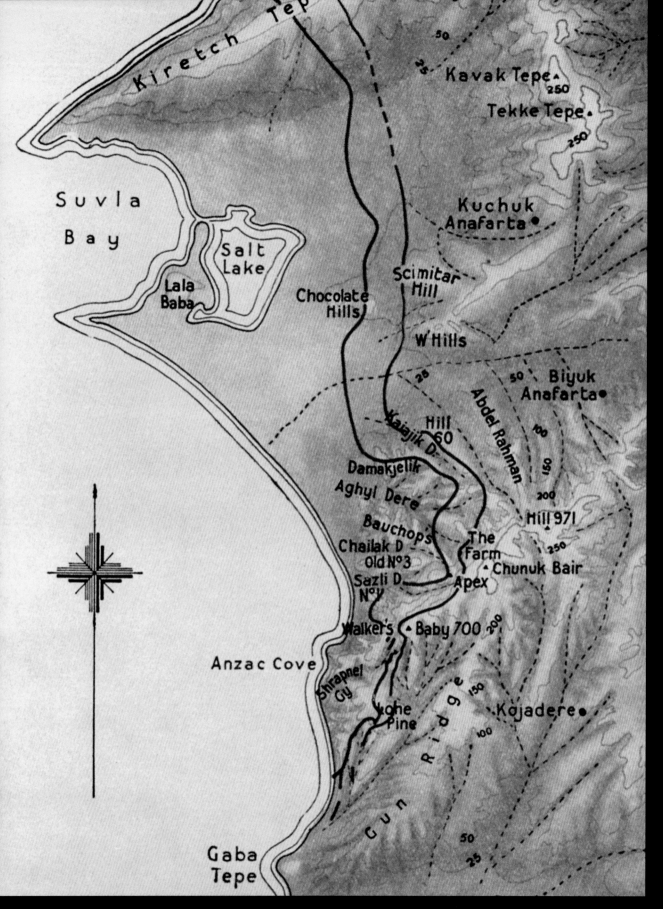

Map shows position of Anzac Cove in relation to the British position to the north at Suvla Bay, August 1915.

Gallipoli campaign as less significant than their victory in driving the British and French fleet from the Dardanelles. The date of that triumph — 18 March 1915 — is emblazoned on a hillside on the Asian side of the great waterway, over the town of Canakkale. The Allies then decided to send a military force, but the Turks had heeded the warning.

Driving down the peninsula, one wonders why the Allies did not attack from the Saros Bay, where the plain might have allowed them a firm grip on the narrow throat of Gallipoli. Perhaps such a course would have been too obvious. The German officer in charge of the defence, General Liman von Sanders, expected the landing there. In any case, the choice of Gaba Tepe as the landing place for the Australians seemed reasonable enough. Defences there were stronger than at Anzac Cove but the land was much flatter. Huseyin Uluaslan, whose father fought in 1915, said: 'If the Australians had landed at Gaba Tepe, it would soon have been all over.'[8] However, the Australians jumped ashore from the boats nearly a mile further north at Anzac Cove. The reason for the mistake has sparked endless speculation. The most common theory was that tides had carried the tows to the north. According to local folklore, a small British landing party had marked Gaba Tepe with covered torches but a Turkish soldier stumbled on the torches and replanted them at the cliffsite where the Anzacs finally landed.[9] The most likely explanation, however, is that the naval ratings lost direction in the dark.

The steepness and unexpected nature of the terrain led to confusion and the inability of the Anzacs to achieve their original objective, the capture of Gun Ridge. By mid-morning the Turkish commander, Mustafa Kemal, who was to become President of Turkey as Kemal Atatürk, was ready to counter-attack. By evening Major-General William Bridges, the Australian commander who was to be fatally wounded three weeks later, recommended evacuation. Lieutenant-General Sir William Birdwood, British commander of the Anzac force, agreed. Hamilton, in the *Queen Elizabeth*, overruled his commanders and ordered the troops to dig in, but the best chance of taking Gallipoli had gone with the day. The deadlock that the invasion was planned to overcome spread to Gallipoli. When the two sides negotiated an armistice on 24 May to bury their dead, the enemies exchanged cigarettes, sweets and souvenirs. Turkish General Fahrettin Altay recalled: 'I saw an Australian soldier who was trying to measure the height of our tallest soldier and our soldier was letting him do so with a smile on his face. As time passed the area was starting to look like a festival place … soon after the armistice ended and the area was covered with noisy explosions and clouds of fire.'

The last concerted Allied attempt to take Gallipoli was launched on 6 August and led to bloodbaths at Lone Pine, the Nek and elsewhere. The futile and botched charge of the demounted Lighthorsemen at the Nek, when they were cut down by the Turks, is etched in the Australian consciousness. Australia's official war historian, C.E.W. Bean, said of Lone Pine: 'The dead lay so thick that the only respect that could be paid to them was to avoid treading on their faces.' After documenting total losses at Gallipoli, he wrote: 'But Anzac stood, and still stands, for reckless valour in a good cause, for enterprise, resourcefulness, fidelity, comradeship, and endurance that will never own defeat.' Yet, in the end, Gallipoli had little or no influence on the course of the war. Even if the Allies had taken the peninsula, Kemal and other Turkish leaders would most likely have mounted a robust defence of Constantinople.[10] Another view is that Allied, essentially British, strategy was fundamentally flawed. Lord Kitchener consistently baulked at assigning enough troops and resources to give it a real chance of achieving success.[11] In any case, Gallipoli was only a mistake because the Allies did not succeed.

There are thirty-one cemeteries on the peninsula. Counts of the casualties vary, but the Australian War Memorial puts the Australian dead at 8,709 and the New Zealand at 2,701. Britain lost nearly four times as many as did Australia. France lost as many. The Turks acknowledged 86,700 dead and 164,000 wounded or sick. But Britain, France and Turkey had, or once had, empires. Australia had been a nation for only fourteen years and many people still thought of the land as a colony. The awful body count meant more to the emerging nation. The fact that it was a first time also detracted from Australian victories on the Western Front, where they broke the German line and helped liberate France and Belgium and where 48,617 Australians died.

There are other areas where the historical fact clouds with legend and fades into myth. Not all the Anzacs were heroes. Sir Robert Rhodes-James, the eminent British historian, has blamed Australian film-makers like Peter Weir and authors like Bert Facey and Alan Moorehead for perpetuating the myth that all Anzacs were brave but doomed soldiers under the command of blundering British officers: 'Not all the British commanders were useless — not all the Anzac officers were competent.'[12] It was an Australian officer, Colonel J.M. Antill, who insisted on the third and fourth lines of Australians rushing to their deaths at the Nek.

It is also difficult to argue that Australia became a nation at Gallipoli when, in fact, the men were responding to British imperial demands. It is more accurate to say that Australia became a nation at Federation in 1901 and the events of Gallipoli marked a turning point in the relationship with Britain. Gavin Souter writes of the returning soldiers: 'They were not the same men who had embarked from Australia a few years before, bound happily for Armageddon; nor were their kinsfolk in Australia quite the same. As the heat of summer hardens a cicada newly emerged from dark years in the ground, so the heat of war might be said to have hardened the Australian sense of identity. The British–Australian sense of duality was still discernible, but not to the same pervasive extent as it had been in 1901.'[13] In a way, Australia behaved much more like a real nation in World War II, when Prime Minister John Curtin baulked at Churchill's demands and brought the troops home to defend Australia.

In any case, as Patsy Adam-Smith says, Australians are born with a legend, like it or not. We can ridicule it, but we cannot rid ourselves of it.

1   Bill Gammage, *The Broken Years*, p 44.
2   Peter Dennis et al, *The Oxford Companion to Australian Military History*, p 262.
3   John Masefield, *Gallipoli*, p 19.
4   Ken Inglis, *Current Affairs Bulletin*, April 1988, p 6.
5   *The Age*, 22 September 1983.
6   Geoffrey Blainey, *The Australian*, 24 April 1990.
7   Barbara Tuchman, *The March of Folly*, p 5.
8   *Sydney Morning Herald*, 25 April 1987.
9   F.J. Fink, letter 20 April 1995 to *Sydney Morning Herald*.
10 Dennis et al, The Oxford Companion to Australian Military History, p 261.
11 Nigel Steel and Peter Hart, *Defeat at Gallipoli*, p 419.
12 *The Australian*, 25 April 1995.

ANZAC: The Men

The human heart is the beginning and end of all matters pertaining to war.
Maréchal de Saxe, 1732

Claude Fankhauser and Roy Longmore.

The first thing to be noticed about these original Anzacs, the men of Gallipoli, was their gentleness and the contrast between this quality and their violent past. You wonder how they managed to be violent. The next thing was their accepting nature. They rarely asked for anything. They accepted their lot in life, just as they did at Gallipoli in 1915. There was still spirit and steel in the old bodies but they accepted their blindness and their deafness, their fragile bones and failing memories.

Their faces betrayed time passing. Nearly 50,000 Australians went to the peninsula and about 18,000 New Zealanders. Around one hundred Anzac originals were alive in 1990, the seventy-fifth anniversary, when about half made the pilgrimage to Gallipoli. By 1996, when the first edition of this book was published, there were probably only twenty-one left. They were all around one hundrded years old. There were three New Zealanders, an Englishman who had joined the

27

Australian Light Horse, and seventeen Australians. When Alec Campbell died in 2002 they had all gone.

One veteran in Western Australia who would never be interviewed about his wars died towards the end of 1995, aged ninety-nine. Eugene Alfred Fathers, having tried Gallipoli and France, then put his age down to go to World War II and ended up a prisoner of war of the Japanese, thus completing a famously hellish double.

Another declined to be interviewed, largely because he refused to wear a hearing aid. Francis (Frank) Isaacs was born in Charters Towers, Queensland, in 1896, left school at twelve and went to Gallipoli with the 49th Battalion. He was wounded on the Western Front at Etaples and blinded in the left eye. Back home, he worked as a bootmaker in Townsville, married Philomena Stapleton and had seven children. He also worked on cattle stations and as a Sydney tram conductor. 'The reason he took little interest in war anniversaries is that he thought war should be forgotten — except when he talked about it,' said his eldest child, Joy Wilson. When he did talk, one of his frequent themes was what he saw as the superiority of the Australian Army. He did not have much time for French troops and voiced his opinion at a French function in his honour. He also liked to talk of how women fell for Gallipoli heroes in France when the Anzacs took leave. 'Oh! You should have seen the clobber of the Froggie sheilas. They looked bonzer.' Records in the National Archives of Australia show that Isaacs faced two courts martial in 1918. He was found not guilty of desertion, but guilty of being absent without leave, on the first. He was found guilty of desertion on the second, when he disappeared in France two months before the end of the war, and was not found until January 1919. His five-year sentence was commuted to one year and he was honourably discharged. After his wife died, he took to travelling round Australia, visiting relatives and friends. He was still doing this in his nineties. His false teeth and medals were stolen from an old people's home in Brisbane and he was mugged in Sydney. Frank finally settled in Perth with Mrs Wilson. 'He's happy reading the newspaper and gardening,' she said. 'And he still sometimes speaks French to confuse people.' Frank Isaacs died in 1999.

Lord Granville of Eye declined approaches in England for an interview. As Edgar Louis Granville, he had found himself at Gallipoli two months after his sixteenth birthday. Born in England, he had joined the Light Horse while on a trip to Australia. 'I remember you had to do a riding test to get in and it was hell's bells,' Lord Granville recalled many years later. The young Granville lost his hat in the process but the recruiting sergeant said: 'Okay, son, you're in.' He was wounded at Gallipoli but recovered to take part in the Light Horse victory at Beersheba and to become aide-de-camp to General Sir Harry Chauvel, commander at Beersheba. He became MP for Eye, Suffolk, in the House of Commons and, later, an independent in the House of Lords. A bay horse and a kangaroo decorated his crest. He died in 1998.

Stanley Charles Quinn, shortly before his one hundredth birthday in 1996, could remember little about Gallipoli other than that he visited with other World War I veterans in 1990. Stan, of Melbourne, suggested the records be consulted. Some records, however, are sketchy and his do not make clear that he served at Gallipoli. Nonetheless, Stan's claim to have served for a short period at Anzac Cove with the 1st Division Artillery Column were accepted by authorities, who awarded him the Anzac Commemorative Medallion. Until 1995 he had visited a Frankston pub for a drink and a bet. He went perkily enough to a nursing home in 1996 but died soon after.

Joseph Lesley Leach died just months short of his one hundredth birthday, in 1997. Born near Greymouth, New Zealand, he enlisted with the Canterbury Infantry Battalion but was never sure why. 'You just signed up and they gave you a shilling,' he said. 'I think I might have bought a glass of beer with mine.' Leach was wounded at Gallipoli and had his skull fractured in a shell-burst on the Western Front. After the war he became a civil engineer and

Len Hall (standing) and Fred Kelly

Pioneer Lane

Erskineville. The sun came round a corner,
and saw, and went. The sun's habitual corner.
Nothing unusual. The air they breathe
rolls out obscenely from the factory chimneys.
Old age. Just that. No more. And an appraisal
of work-years wasting in these sunless narrows
of terrace-streets which close themselves away,
rejecting newness like the baby stifled
by Leagues Club widows and the warm indifference
of public bars, and traffic loud and poisonous.
Day is so stale; sit in the sun; let it
warm away your questions. Things seem better
in the sun, even when you are old,
as old as these — or so we think — or almost.
Their retribution comes beyond the grave.
Not savage or pretentiously hostile,
they'll gather round, these veterans of Lone Pine
and Villers-Bret. and Passchendaele and Ypres,
a circle close with friendship; and there'll be
no pension-degradation; they'll be free,
these pensioners who made Australia
and fought to keep it, time on bitter time,
a place they could grow old in, never thinking
they'd be despised for even that senescence.
They think I know, of those who stayed behind
in the warm ridges of Gallipoli,
or Flanders mud. A cigarette-smoke circle,
two coins tossed high into the endless year,
falling to choruses of 'Jesus Christ'.

Michael Dransfield

then ran businesses. He married Beth, an Australian, at seventy and they lived in Auckland before moving to Port Macquarie. Returned services organisations in New Zealand lost touch with him, until the *Sydney Morning Herald* located him in a suburban nursing home. He was puzzled by the interest in him and his history, but proud of his powers of survival. 'Only two New Zealanders left?' he said. 'Go on!' A stepson, Greg Adcock, took him on Saturdays to watch his grandson play soccer and the old man took an occasional beer. He had no illusions about immortality. 'I suppose I'm one of the last because I was very young when I joined up,' he said. He had enlisted at sixteen.

In the strict sense, Cyril Checchi was not an Anzac. Yet he was one of the first Australians to answer Britain's call and he served at Gallipoli. The son of an Italian couple, he graduated in medicine from Melbourne University, sailed to England early in 1915, joined Britain's Royal Medical Corps and landed at Cape Helles in September. Because he wanted to serve with the Australians, he had to come home after Gallipoli to re-enlist. He married Frances, 'the magnificent woman who shared my life for sixty-eight years', joined the 18th Battalion as a captain and spent his first wedding anniversary in the mud of the Western Front. In his memoirs published in 1995, Dr Checchi devoted just a few pages to the war and said his greatest joy was serving the people of Willaura, in western Victoria, as a doctor. He was still working in his early nineties, until Parkinson's disease started to affect him, and the authorities refused to renew his driving licence, a decision which annoyed him immensely. He later lived in the hostel at the district hospital he helped build. He died there in 1997, aged 104.

To the survivors, the Australia and New Zealand they knew in 1915 and the Australia and New Zealand near the turn of the century were like foreign countries. A new world had been created, beyond their imaginations in 1915. One had been sold as a slave before dashing off to Gallipoli. Another looked forward to being one of the very few people to live across three centuries, the 19th, 20th and 21st. They all still used words and phrases like 'hell's bells', 'bonzer', 'chum', 'chap', 'by jove', 'blood worth bottling', 'our crowd' and 'geek', meaning look. They spoke of 'that blessed old war' and 'go out' or 'go under', meaning to be killed. They called Gallipoli 'a stunt' and said the battle was 'a very interesting contest'.

They knew towards the end of their lives that they were feted as much for their age as the fact that they had fought at Gallipoli. They had become accidental celebrities through the link between their longevity and a war on the other side of the world nearly a century ago. In a way, they were continuing to serve their country, bearing witness to the mates who died there.

It must have been hard for the last few, and for their families. Their dying had been so public. Australia had counted them off, one by one. Alec Campbell's widow, Kate, had said in 2001, when Roy Longmore's death left her husband as the last Anzac survivor of Gallipoli, that she had dreaded the day. Alec Campbell had become national property. 'I'm not sure Alec realises it — the attention that goes with it,' she said. 'It can be quite dreadful.' The old men put up with the attention, however, usually uncomplaining. They used their ebbing years to ram home the message that most battlefields are unsatisfactory places to resolve arguments. Nearly all spoke out about the folly of war.

Campbell, like most of the old diggers, had considered himself an ordinary soldier, then an ordinary ex-serviceman, for about seventy years. Then, when Australians took a renewed interest in the Anzac story towards the end of the 1980s, many of these men felt it their duty to return to service and try to explain Gallipoli. They were doing in life what the unknown soldier, reburied in the Australian War Memorial in 1993, might continue to do. The prime minister, Paul Keating, said at the time: 'It is not too much to hope that this unknown Australian soldier might continue to serve his country.'

The details of their stories changed a little along the way. Ted Matthews, the last survivor of the Australians to land at Gallipoli on 25 April 1915 — what Manning Clark called 'that sad Sabbath morn' — said in 1995 that he had not fired a shot on the peninsula, where he was a signaller. A few years later he was saying he had fired a shot and hoped he had missed. Alec Campbell said in 1996 that he had not fired a shot. On Anzac Day 2002 he said he had lost count of the number of Turks he had shot. It is possible that the two men's memories were playing tricks. It is just as likely that they had tired of the same questions and were changing their answers in protest. Campbell grew tired of pointing out in his last years that his brief time at Gallipoli was a very small part of his rich life. Longmore's great-granddaughter, sixteen-year-old Carly Longmore, made the point at his funeral service in Melbourne: 'Roy Longmore was the very essence of modesty, humanity, sacrifice, survival and courage. It is unbelievable to think that Roy has lived in three different centuries and had to live with eighty-seven years of graphic memories of those bloody battles of war. Eighty-seven years of waking up every morning and continuing life as normal, eighty-seven years of being nothing less than a hero, eighty-seven years of never once complaining of it.'

The quiet courage of Private John Simpson Kirkpatrick and his donkey at Gallipoli, carrying wounded men to safety under fire, is well known. The frightening feat of Lance-Corporal Albert Jacka, who attacked a Turkish trench singlehanded, killed nine men and won the Victoria Cross, is reasonably well known. Yet most of the Anzacs just dug in and hung on. Some of the old survivors still criticised the politicians who sent them and one or two of the commanders, but they felt admiration for, rather than enmity towards, the old foe. They felt bitterness towards nobody. They knew there was no progress in bitterness.

Some had enlisted out of dutiful patriotism, some out of an innocent sense of adventure, some to escape boredom or poverty. These men who had survived the war and the daunting cliffs had also survived the peace. Several lost their homes in the Great Depression, but they survived that, too. Nearly all their marriages were long and, by all accounts, happy. Some men came home physically broken or psychologically crippled, in the days before counselling. But the last Anzacs had packed up their troubles in old kit bags and nothing seemed too much of a trouble after that.

When Alec Campbell died, his widow Kate was left with thirty-three grandchildren, thirty-five great-grandchildren and two great-great-grandchildren. At the funeral, the widow, the ten proud Campbell women pallbearers, Alec's sixty other direct descendants and another seventy members of their families brought a fresh clarity to the Anzac legend. They demonstrated dramatically the extent of Australia's losses in World War I. The nation lost 8,709 men at Gallipoli and 48,617 in France and Belgium. Campbell survived to produce his admirable clan. What might all those other young men have achieved for the young nation? Alec Campbell had asked the question often. One of his six daughters, Caithleen (Sam) Claridge, said in her eulogy in St David's Cathedral, Hobart, that her father didn't talk much about war but that he marched on Anzac Day 'for the young men claimed by the Gallipoli campaign'.

The hearts and souls of these men, then, remain the heart and soul of Australia. They were fatalists who strove against the oppression of death, historian Bill Gammage says. The survivors all scoffed at the suggestion that they were heroes. A couple, though, remembered the words of General Sir Ian Hamilton: 'Before the war, who had ever heard of Anzac? Hereafter, who will ever forget it?' Some people argue that, now Australia has emerged as a nation, Anzac Day would be best forgotten. It was at best an honourable draw, at worst a defeat, an eight-month sideshow to the Western Front. But Australians couldn't forget Anzac Day if they tried, not even now that the last of the old men have gone.

Jack Buntine

1895–1998
8th Light Horse

Jack Buntine's mother died when he was nine and his drunkard father sold him a year later to a German couple who wanted his labour in their market gardens at Lakes Entrance, Victoria. The woman, he said, beat him, so he threw her to the ground, knocking her out. Young Jack fled to the bush, took up with an Aborigine, Percy Pepper, who treated him as a son, and worked swinging a hammer in a blacksmith's shop, labelling bottles in a brewery, as a painter, droving sheep and boundary riding around Nyngan and Lake Cargelligo in western New South Wales. His elder brother Perce, who had tried to look after Jack and three other young siblings, went off to war in 1914 and Jack joined the 8th Light Horse. 'The family was split up to billy-o,' he said. 'I was very pleased to go to Gallipoli.'

He fell on the troopship, fracturing his pelvis in three places and damaging discs in his spine, but resisted attempts to send him home. 'I wasn't fit but they couldn't stop me.' He fought as a sniper on the peninsula, having learnt to shoot as a boy of eleven. 'I could hit a jam tin at eight hundred yards. I was just doing a job.'

Enteric fever ended his time at Gallipoli. In hospital in England he sang songs, accompanied by his friend, Jack Cam, on piano. Then he went to the Middle East in a signals company, became a batman until he deliberately tipped soup down the officer's neck and went to France as a driver with a 4th Division artillery unit, 'pushing Fritz up the line'.

In 1918 he drove machine guns and ammunition to soldiers on the Western Front. Arriving at the front,

he was told to use his truck to rescue wounded soldiers, driving round the battlefield and crawling along the trenches to pick up the suffering. He won the Military Medal on 8 August 1918, for conspicuous bravery and devotion to duty at Morcourt — delivering stores and rescuing men while under continuous fire. 'You didn't lift the blanket,' he said of mates who died.

When the Armistice was signed, Jack Buntine was drinking tea near Boulogne. 'When we heard it, we kept on drinking tea. We didn't give a damn. Oh, that's a great memory, yes.' Yet war had given him a sense of importance, that he was carrying out important, even vital, work as part of a team.

Back home, he couldn't sleep in a house. He went trapping and shooting and fossicked for gold. 'In the army, when you wanted money, you went to the quartermaster. When you wanted food, you went to the quartermaster. When I got back I was hopeless. It took me a while to straighten out.' Later on he taught himself to play the violin by ear. He sat down and read war histories, trying to find the answers to the horrors and discovering that Germans and Turks were just as much victims as Australians. By the time a grandson, John Reid, married Melinda, a woman with German parents, Jack Buntine had exorcised his hatred of Germans.

He settled down with marriage in 1925 but his first wife died from peritonitis when she was thirty-one, leaving him with two little girls. He married Jean Findlay and had four more children, the last at sixty years. By 1996, Jack and Jean Buntine had been married for fifty-nine years and had nineteen grandchildren and twenty-two great-grandchildren. He still played occasionally with the great-grandchildren. Enid Reid, a daughter, said: 'He was always very good with children. He encouraged us to look after our little ones. That's what was most respected, much more than winning at sport or at school.'

On his one hundredth birthday in 1995, Jack's family hired a church hall in Melbourne and filled it with friends and relatives. The youngest generation, like his great-granddaughter Virginia Holdenson, nineteen months old, was there. He had Anzac Day lunch that year in a Turkish restaurant, bearing witness for those who died and knowing that Anzac is more to do with mateship and sacrifice than power and conquest.

He was contacted soon after by the Department of Veterans' Affairs and told that a decoration allowance introduced in 1975 entitled him to a small payment. The backdated sum came to a little over $1,000. 'I didn't know anything about it,' the old soldier said. 'It came as a pleasant surprise.'

Jack Buntine had no plans for the money. He said, however: 'I look forward to a quiet life. I have a few things left to do. Then I can pass out, I hope.' He will be remembered most for the deeds of his youth and early manhood but his family remembers him differently. Nearly all his children, grandchildren and great-grandchildren visited him in his last week. 'He asked us all to kiss him,' said Enid Reid, a daughter. 'He knew he had lived long enough. We are very lucky to have had such a wonderful man for a father. His early life taught him the value of the family.'

Jack Buntine with his great-granddaughter, Virginia Holdenson.

Alec Campbell

1899–2002

15th Battalion Reinforcements

Alec Campbell will be remembered as a soldier, the last Anzac or, more precisely, the last Australian survivor of Gallipoli. He had accepted the description long before his death but didn't like it much. His wife, Kate, had accepted it, too, and liked it even less. Campbell had known that Gallipoli took less than a year of his life, less than one per cent of a lifetime. There was much more to his rich and happy life than the small part he played in a famous battle in a famous war over empires on the other side of the world.

He was born into a farming family, a colonial before Federation formally made Australians of the white people who lived on this continent. In Canberra in 1927, when the first Parliament House was being built, he was building homes for public servants and others. He earned an economics degree after he turned fifty. He fathered the last of his nine children at sixty-nine. He sailed in six Sydney-to-Hobart yacht races and circumnavigated Tasmania in the sloop Kintail. He was president of the Launceston Trades Hall Council, campaigned with Lady Jessie Street for peace and contributed to the *Australian Dictionary of Biography*. While many old soldiers remember war as the high point of their lives, Campbell said a few years before he died: 'Cripes, Gallipoli was a significant event in history but it is not all that important personally.' When Roy Longmore died, leaving Alec as the last Gallipoli veteran, he said in his Hobart home: 'That won't last forever. I don't feel special. I'm an ordinary man.'

Alec and Kate Campbell.

Born in Launceston, Campbell was working as an insurance clerk before enlisting at sixteen years and four months and joining reinforcements for the 15th Battalion. He wasn't even shaving. 'I must have lied,' he said. 'It was necessary to put my age up if I wanted to go and everyone was going. A lot of us went and a lot didn't come back. You don't look for reasons. It's all a bit of adventure at that age. Egypt was like a fairyland but I suppose we had some idea of protecting Australia and England.'

His mother and father acquiesced unhappily. Campbell recalled well into his nineties his mother walking along the dock before his ship sailed, her silent steps hinting at the hurt in her heart. He landed at Gallipoli in late November. Veterans called him 'the kid' and tried to look after him. He was made a water boy, carrying blocks of ice from the beach to the men in the front lines. He recalled a colleague being shot before their boat had landed on the now famous beach. He remembered a leg sticking out of a bush on Hill 60, although he could not have been part of the savage fighting there in August which took such a heavy toll on the 15th and other battalions under General John Monash. 'It kept you on your toes,' Alec said in 1997. 'To stick up your noodle was nearly always fatal.'

He also remembered seeing Lord Kitchener walking on the beach at Anzac Cove. 'I can still see this big, tall bloke with stooped shoulders walking up and down in front of us, as we stood under the big Anzac sign on the beach, saying we were as fine a group as ever sent.' Young Campbell went down with influenza and was discharged from his hospital tent on 19 December, the last day before the last of the Anzacs were evacuated in darkness.

He never killed anyone. He said in 1990, before returning to Gallipoli with other old soldiers for the seventy-fifth anniversary: 'It was a beautiful place, you know, if it hadn't been in different circumstances. The sea was beautiful and the little beach at Anzac Cove was a pretty little beach and the steep hills and the background and the Sphinx, standing up high above the others. The landing was awful. I can remember now, the first fellow that I saw hit. He was on the ship, actually, getting into the boats. And I think that shocked me more than a lot of others that I saw because it was the first one and he was hit in the head … Oh, there were a lot of young fellows on the peninsula. I didn't get there until after the big August attack and it was mainly a holding operation the rest of the time I was there. There were casualties from Turkish snipers and the shellfire. The Turkish guns were very accurate with the shrapnel shelling. And their rifle shooting was accurate. If you exposed yourself in any way you were likely to get hit. I am not a philosopher. Gallipoli was Gallipoli. That's all there was about it. Once we were there, we didn't expect to survive.'

After the war, he worked as a jackaroo, a carriage builder, a carpenter and with the railways around Australia. After World War II, he took his economics degree and joined the Department of Labour and National Service. In the 1999 referendum, he voted for an Australian republic. 'I believe it's time we took the final step and had one of our own as head of state,' he said. His vote flew in the face of a public perception that all old soldiers were fighters for the status quo and, therefore, the monarchy.

He married twice, first Kathleen Connolly and, after a divorce, Kathleen Corvan. He had seven children from his first marriage and two from his second, three sons and six daughters. His nine children, including two doctors of philosophy, have all led successful lives. The children remember him as politically left, enthusiastic about trade unions and sympathetic to the Fabian Society. W.A. 'Mick' Townsley, a professor of political science in Tasmania, remembered him talking about the possibility of going to the Spanish Civil War to fight against Franco. The family recall his 'lust for life', mending shoes, milking cows, panning for gold, reading books about politics, philosophy and the origin of the species. He built boats in the backyard, boxed, shot pheasants, taught the children how to swim and to play marbles, read them *The Last of the Mohicans* and took them for walks in the bush. Some recall his reciting bawdy poems such as 'Abdul el Bulbul Emir'.

The Campbells had not much wanted a state funeral. They decided, however, that they would complete the patriarch's last tour of duty. Women are often neglected on such occasions, even when war made them widows or when their men came home so bruised that life became intolerable. The Campbells did not let that happen. Alec had insisted, after all, that all his children receive good educations and grow up to think for themselves. The Campbell clan therefore reclaimed their man at the funeral, making it not so much a matter of state as a family funeral on a grand scale.

Nonetheless, Prime Minister John Howard spoke of 'the respect we feel and the debt we owe to this grand old man and those he came to represent. Within his generation can be found much of the richness of this nation's history. Within this one life are illustrated the living values that transformed Australia from the hopeful young federation of Alec's childhood to one of the great developed nations of the modern era.' Howard said that young Australians drew strength from the Anzac story. And he paid tribute to the way in which Alec Campbell had shouldered 'the weight of history imposed upon him' in his old age. The Prime Minister bowed to the coffin.

Doug Dibley

1896–1997

New Zealand Mounted Corps

Doug Dibley, born in Wellington, recalled his New Zealand childhood, fishing in the Cook Strait and 'eating mutton for breakfast, dinner and tea'. When spinal meningitis broke out in New Zealand, Doug went to hospital with a cobber, offering help. Instead, he was signed up by the Mounted Medical Corps. He told his parents: 'They are going to send us overseas.' He said in 1995: 'There was nothing much said. We had no idea what we were going for.'

The Mounted Corps left their horses in Egypt. Doug was a stretcher-bearer at Gallipoli, toiling for a time at Walker's Ridge, and being evacuated on the last day. 'It wasn't a lot of fun. The Turks were firing all the time.' Eighty years later he was more interested in talking about his post-war achievements as a farmer or investor. He still did his own banking and kept files marked 'Inland Revenue', 'Investments' and 'Bank Correspondence'.

Yet he offered a diary written by Sapper Arthur Bellingham, of the New Zealand Field Engineers, who met up with his younger brother, Ernest, and landed at Gallipoli on 25 April, when he wrote presciently: 'It looks like a very difficult position to attack.' And, on 1 May: 'Gee! I can't write down all that has happened during this terrible week. I must give up the idea of keeping this diary as it's worse than hell to think of the horrible sights we see every day …'

May 18: 'Gee! I am a lucky begga (sic). Bullets were landing on the track quite close all the way up. I got a smack in the leg. By jove! It did sting but luckily it did not go in. It must have hit the bank and bounced off onto me … I found Ernie in a dugout. Just in time for breakfast.'

May 20: 'Orders came right along the whole line to cease fire and in a few minutes not a shell could be heard except the big naval guns away over in the Narrows. Our men hopped up out of their trenches to have a look at the Turks who were doing the same. The interpreters with white flags were having a conflab (sic) between the trenches … Gee! It was a wonderful change. The quiet after a month of hard fighting. I believe there was more excitement during that lull than when the firing was on. The truce lasted till nearly dark when suddenly the firing broke out louder than I've ever heard before. The noise was terrific — it sounded like the world was coming to an end … Gee Whittaker! I'll never forget that night as long as I live.'

May 24: 'Today has been a very exciting one for us. An armistice was declared from 7.30 this morning to 4.30 pm for the purpose of burying the dead … The Turks and our men were talking together and exchanged cigarettes. It does seem to me to be a peculiar world in which we live when we cannot think of any other way of settling disputes, without murdering one another.'

Doug Dibley 'went looking for ruins' in the Middle East before transferring to the New Zealand Field Ambulance and going to France, where he

Doug Dibley in pith helmet far right.

contracted spinal meningitis. This was where his war had begun. Now it was ending. He recovered in hospital in England and went home.

He farmed sheep and cows near Rotorua, married Susanna Karl, a Yugoslav, and had eleven children. At last count, there were fifty-two grandchildren and more than eighty great-grandchildren. He served in the Home Guard in World War II but, like many other returned servicemen, opposed wars. 'The Great War took the best of our young men, and look how many came back maimed and broken,' he said. 'Many suffered dreadfully for the rest of their lives.' He drove a car until he was ninety-eight, when he started baking his own bread. 'I'm a funny sort of a chap. I get on with the chaps but I'm a bit of an individualist. I went to a lunch at the Returned Services' Association club but thought I didn't want to sit around with those old chaps.'

He didn't go back. Instead, he read large-type books with a magnifying glass or listened to talking books or classical music, Beethoven, Mozart, Schubert. He wondered about some modern literature: 'The language and the sex. Good Lord!' His Christian faith ran deep. 'The good Lord has been very good to me but I hope the next place is even better than this.'

Tom Epps

1897–1997

27th Battalion

Tom Epps put his age up to go to war. His father, Henry, then aged forty-seven, put his down. They ended up in the same Cyclists Battalion in France. 'Dad was wounded in the bum and they woke up to his age,' Tom said. 'My brother Cecil was in the 10th Battalion when a bullet hit him in the head. He died young. Then my boy, Charles, was killed in the air force in World War II. He was only nineteen and a half.'

Tom had little to thank war for. He said Gallipoli was 'the greatest mess ever, made by old generals'. An apprentice compositor, he enlisted partly 'because behind the whole business was the idea of getting round the world. Enlistment was voluntary, of course, but there was prejudice against those who didn't enlist. If you didn't go, you were looked down on as being a bit windy.'

Tom sailed with the 27th Battalion on 1 April 1915 — 'I'll never forget the date' — arriving five days before his eighteenth birthday. He survived three months in the trenches under the hills of Sari Bair, held by the Turks. Wounded when a spent bullet fell from the sky, went through his boot and into his left

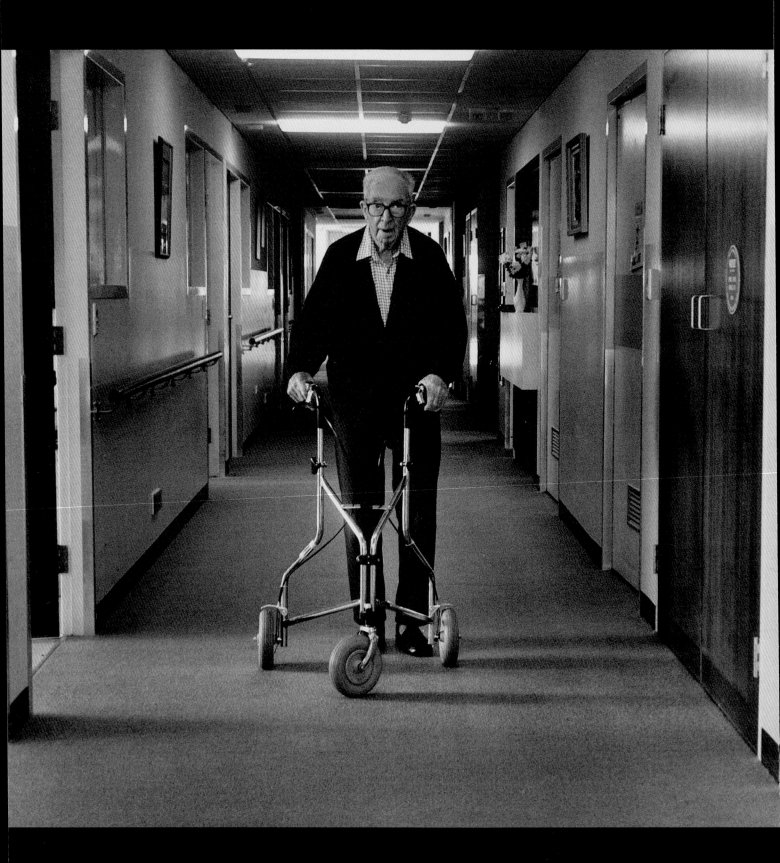

foot, he spent a week recovering with the 1st Ambulance on the beach. 'That was the only real dodge I had. I was lucky. Our men weren't shot up like the first wave, although five hundred were taken off with dysentery and yellow jaundice.'

After evacuation he fought on the Western Front in France and Belgium. He fought at Bullecourt, where the Australians suffered 7,000 casualties. He was on a battlefield in Belgium when the guns fell silent at 11am on 11 November 1918. 'Remembrance Day and Anzac Day should be lessons to us,' he said. 'They are not days about the glory of war or about nationalism but a lesson in the futility of war. I was brainless, but I'm not sorry I went. It taught me how stupid the politicians and military can be. They were boneheads. The 1914–18 war was mass murder. Ninety-nine per cent of war is stupid.'

He went to Westminster Abbey for the seventieth anniversary service in 1985 and with the Australian contingent to Gallipoli in 1990, 'to see the place in peacetime'. He felt no lasting enmity to his old foes but his contempt for politicians and generals for having begun what he saw as an exercise in futility did not diminish with the years. 'If there is no other way of settling arguments, the human race should be exterminated.'

After the war Tom had trouble settling down. He returned to work as a compositor, then joined the public service, looking for work to take his mind off the war. Gradually the pain subsided, even if the anger remained. Marriage in 1923 to Ada Matilda Stone, always called Till from her second name, helped his recovery. Till was raised in the bush on traditional values: home, family, school, church. She kept a copy of the New Testament presented to schoolchildren to commemorate the coronation of King George V. She wrote on the flyleaf: 'I have promised to read this every day of my life — Tillie Stone.'

Tom and Till had five children but lost their house in the Depression and suffered again when Charles died in World War II. When Till had a stroke, and a son, Jack, gave up work to look after the couple, Tom finally decided to put himself in a nursing home because Jack couldn't cope with them both and Till couldn't cope with the idea of a nursing home. She died in 1994, after seventy-one years of marriage, and twenty-one great-grandchildren. He missed her but he had long grown to accept the inevitability of death. He had seen his mates die at war and in peace. He had outlived all his 27th Battalion comrades. When Jack said he missed his mother, the old soldier said: 'These things happen, Jack, and you have to accept them.'

Nonetheless, he talked about living to 103 so that he would be one of the few people to live in three centuries. He still liked to attend Anzac Day services — 'But I won't do anything stupid this time.' He still dreamt about Gallipoli — 'Occasionally I have a dream … not often … just occasionally. I dream I'm back over there.' He enjoyed outings with his family from the nursing home where he lived but liked to be back home by 4.30pm because this was the time his pre-dinner beer was opened. One of the nurses, Barbara Aleksic, from Serbia, said he was a 'lovely, lovely man'. The lovely man chided her: 'The Great War started in the Balkans and you lot are still arguing the point. I wonder whether the human race will one day wear itself out.'

Claude Fankhauser
1895–1996
5th Battalion

Claude Augustus Leopold Fankhauser never had much time for those carefree, youthful days. His family had come to Australia seeking religious freedom and he remembered vaguely, in 1996, the celebrations for Federation and the mourning for Queen Victoria's death, both in 1901. He left school at fourteen to work in the family orchard in suburban Melbourne, before joining a Camberwell coachbuilder — horse coaches, that is. He had to walk three miles to the railway station to catch a steam train to work. 'I ran mostly because I was always late.'

Just a few years later, and a few days after his twenty-first birthday, Claude was blinded totally in fighting on the Somme. He had tried to enlist immediately after war broke out, 'of course'. He was rejected the first time 'because my heart wasn't too good … I think I was a bit excited.' His heart apparently beat more regularly in January 1915, when he was accepted into D Company of the 5th Battalion.

He arrived at Gallipoli via Egypt in July, three days after his twentieth birthday, and spent six months in the trenches, mainly in Shrapnel Gully and later at Lone Pine. 'We were roughly in the thick of it. The Turks were just over the brow of the hill. You didn't put your head up too high. We may have shouted abuse but they probably didn't understand and we certainly didn't understand them. Kitchener said we didn't win the war but we kept the Turkish Army occupied. He called us gentlemen. I thought that was a bit funny.'

In conversation with the Reverend Lindsay Faulkner, a friend who wrote a monograph on Fankhauser, Claude recalled going down to the beach for supplies: 'I remember picking my way over these cobblestones to get to the water and I heard a shell coming and I think I did it in two strides back under the embankment.'

Evacuated to Egypt, Claude swam the Suez Canal. 'I always remember. We were on the Asian side. They were a bit worried that the Turks would advance through Palestine and attack. My swim took me from Asia to Africa.' His next stop was Europe, and the mud and the blood of the Somme.

His whole battalion, about a thousand men, was sent forward at Pozières on the night of 25 July 1916. 'Only one hundred-odd came out. It was slaughter. I was one of the wounded. I came face to face with a hand grenade … My face was scattered with bits. I haven't seen since.' The Australian 1st Division suffered 5,285 casualties in seventy-two hours. The 2nd Division lost 6,846 men, killed, wounded or missing during fourteen days around Pozières. Finally, after seven weeks fighting in the area, Australian casualties were put at 23,300. It was more than the total losses at Gallipoli.

Claude convalesced in England, returned to Australia and then went back to St Dunstan's, an English hostel working for men and women blinded in the services. He learnt braille and carpentry and took up rowing on the Thames. Collecting a pile of braille books on returning to Australia, he complained they were 'full of murder and sex'.

Claude met the woman who was to be his wife, Elsie Littlewood, at St Dunstan's. She was a nursing aide and returned to Australia with him. When she developed tuberculosis, Claude built a house at Blackburn because what is now the suburb was then considered part of the countryside. Elsie died there in 1926, leaving Claude and their son of four and a half years, Frank. Blind father and toddler son made the long journey to England so Elsie's family could see the boy.

Back in Australia, Claude turned his backyard into an orchard and vegetable garden, with poultry sheds on the side. He played cribbage with cards marked in braille and taught people like Lindsay Faulkner how to fish. He was one of those selected to return to Gallipoli on the seventy-fifth anniversary in 1990. An X-ray taken at the time revealed pieces of metal embedded in his cheek, chin and neck. In 1996 he still lived alone in the big suburban house, accepting Meals on Wheels and occasional help from housekeepers but asking for nothing. His living room was scattered with family photographs he did not see. His son Frank, grandson Dr Stephen Fankhauser and great-grandson visited regularly. After a period in hospital he was resisting attempts to place him in a nursing home. 'I've lived here for quite a while, you know.' He had lived there for nearly seventy-five years.

He thanked callers for taking the time to visit, but the thanks were due to Mr Fankhauser. Was his name German?

'Austrian.'

Thomas Gray
1896–1996
4th Light Horse

Thomas Gray enlisted in the 4th Light Horse from a wheat and sheep farm — to protect Australia, for the money and excitement and because girls admired young men in uniform. Gallipoli was a different world. The only point Gallipoli had in common with the little villages around Pyramid Hill in Victoria where young Tom lived was that they were battlefields for survival. The people of the Victorian countryside were pioneers of one sort, the Anzacs of Gallipoli pioneers of another.

Tom had little formal education because he had to walk about six kilometres to school, usually barefooted because shoes or boots were meant for show. He would put them on at the school gate, having saved the leather. His father was a strict disciplinarian. Children were seen, but not heard. If Tom was found to have offended against the rules of the house he would be required to break a switch from a tree and take it to the father, who administered what he saw as appropriate punishment.

So the young man went willingly from an unknown place called Mologa to the troop ship that was to take him to the historic site called Gallipoli, touched with patriotism but fired with the chance to escape the monotony of rural life and broaden his horizons. The young man who would have been lost in Melbourne climbed the pyramids, marvelled at the Sphinx and explored the streets of Cairo. He spoke frequently of all this in later years, and of the beauty of London and his visits to Glasgow, the city of his forefathers.

He spoke less happily of Gallipoli, its horrors and the mates he lost there. Pressed, he spoke of the landing, when he had to hold his rifle above his head because the water came up to his neck. He could hear 'the bastard bullets whizzing around your head'. He told of his first night in the trenches, wondering why his choice of a sleeping spot had not been taken by others and discovering next morning that he had slept on the mass grave of Turkish soldiers. He spoke a little of bravery and of people like Simpson and his donkey, but he did not tell what it was like to shoot another human being. No one asked. Tom Gray served in France and, at the end of the war, 'laid the fellas out in the morgue. It wasn't much of a job.'

Back home and planning to be an engineer, he studied at the Royal Melbourne Institute of Technology, taking extra lectures in philosophy and health, dancing at the Green Mill, rowing on the Yarra, playing tennis at Albert Park and golf at Yarra Bend, until his mother called him back to the farm. 'It was in the days when young men did what their mothers told them,' said Patricia English, his daughter. He didn't enjoy farming but he used his engineering training to invent farming appliances, some of which are on display in the Pyramid Hill museum.

He married Eileen Harte late, at thirty-nine, and Tom and Eileen went to live in the mud brick house he had built for her. It still stood around the turn of the century. Mrs Gray always said that her years there were the happiest of her life. They had two children but Depression and drought pushed the family off the farm. He worked during World War II in an armaments factory. At home in Maidstone, Melbourne, he made things for his family — a penny-farthing bike, billy-carts, scooters, doll's houses. He played the saw, tin whistle and button accordion and took the neighbourhood children to the museum, the zoo and Luna Park. He repaid the loan on the house when he was eighty-two. He coached tennis until he was eighty-six, his players including the children of refugees from another war, in Vietnam.

Tom and Eileen had five great-grandchildren. His attitude to children was determined by his own upbringing. Physical punishment was not his way. The children were encouraged to discuss their points of view.

Eileen Gray died in the nursing home where Tom also lived and, for a long while, he would not walk past her door. He thought he had had enough of life, until he took up woodwork, at ninety-two. He was profoundly deaf, an after-effect of the noise of the guns, but liked to read newspaper headlines every day and was happy to answer questions written down. His face still lit up when he re-read postcards written by girlfriends he'd met on leave in Britain. He still had a glass of port before lunch.

Patricia English said: 'I feel sad when I hear him say that he does not think he would like to live his life over again, but I can easily understand his sentiments.' As for the war, Tom Gray had last words: 'It's like a time set apart — just a big blank that doesn't join up with private life at all.'

Len Hall

1897–1999

10th Light Horse

Leonard Francis Hall joined the 10th Light Horse Regiment in that blackest month, August 1914. He was only sixteen years and five months old but his regiment needed a bugler. His service number was fifty-two. Built like a jockey, he was a good horseman. The boy gave a girl he scarcely knew an emu plume from his hat before he left. Back home in 1919, a young woman stopped him in the street, introduced herself as Eunice Lydiate and said: 'Excuse me, may I give you back your plume?' They were married in 1921, and were together until Eunice died at the end of 1995.

Len was born in Burwood, NSW, and educated in New Zealand until the age of twelve, when he went to Western Australia with his father to buy wheat. He was 'young and foolish', working for a grocer when war broke out. When Major Clive Nicholas discovered that his 10th Light Horse was without a bugler and that young Hall could play the instrument, Nicholas put the boy's age up. Even so, there must have been a problem. His jockey size might have been a factor. Len asked his father to give permission for his enlistment. Mr Hall wrote from Nugarin, Western Australia, on 25 January 1915, to a Captain Todd: '… am writing to say that he has my full & free permission to go & hope that he will do his duty & return safely …'

It was a sense of duty, then, probably not far removed from patriotism. Hall sailed off to war and never played his bugle. 'We went because we were called to protect Australia,' he said. He went ashore under the cover of darkness and under fire. Men of the 10th Light Horse were used as infantry at Lone Pine, Walker's Ridge and the Nek. He served as a machine-gunner during the infamously mad and horrible charge on the Turkish trenches at the Nek.

Men of the 10th followed two waves of 8th Light Horse who were annihilated. 'Boys, you have ten minutes to live,' said the 10th's commanding officer. At the end of the day 375 of the 600 attackers were casualties.

Historian C.E.W. Bean wrote: 'The West Australians assumed that death was certain, and each in the secret places of his mind debated how he would go to it. Mate, having said good-bye to mate … went forward to meet death instantly, running as straight and swiftly as they could at the Turkish rifles. With that regiment went the flower of the youth of Western Australia … the Nek could be seen crowded with the bodies of the Light Horse men … Over the whole summit the figures lay still in the quivering heat.'

Len Hall, the last of the 10th, said: 'We were supposed to fire over their heads but it was impossible. It was stunning. One man crawled back the next day but everyone else in the charge was dead.' Len was one of the last men off Gallipoli. 'The evacuation was the only successful part of the campaign.' He never smoked or took alcohol, except when Royal Navy sailors forced rum down his throat to keep him warm during the evacuation.

In the Middle East, he met Lawrence of Arabia, rode victorious into Damascus with the 10th and represented Australian troops at Easter services in the Church of the Holy Sepulchre, Jerusalem. Obituaries in 1999 noted that young Hall had recovered from the trauma of Gallipoli in time to help capture Beersheba in 1917 in the — this time famous — charge of the Light Horse. However, the Beersheba charge of 31 October was made by the 4th and 12th Light Horse regiments of the 4th Australian Light Horse Brigade. At this time Hall was in the 3rd Machine Gun Squadron of the 3rd Brigade, fighting for Tel el Saba, five kilometres east of Beersheba. German bombs killed nine of the fourteen men in his gun crew, and several of their horses. Hall, wounded in the arms and shoulders, always said that he had been saved by his horse, which took the brunt of one explosion. Sir Sidney Kidman, the Australian pastoralist known as the 'Cattle King' who donated fighter planes and other items to the armed forces, provided Len's bay horse, called Q6 after the Kidman brand. 'He was a wonderful horse. He wouldn't let anyone else on him. I was talking to him, as we all did, just before he was hit.' The old lighthorseman still believed that horses would have helped a landing at Suvla Bay in 1915.

Returning to Australia, Len rejoined the grocery business, before becoming a telephone technician. He and Eunice, the girl who waited with the plume, had three children and 'plenty of grandchildren and great-grandchildren'. He said: 'I have believed over the years that the law of compensation is always with us. Age may rob us of agility but gives us a wealth of memories.'

He nursed Eunice for fifteen years before she entered a nursing home with Alzheimer's disease. He cooked and cleaned for himself but said: 'It's pretty lonely without the boss.' He visited her three times a week until her death, a three-hour round trip by public transport. He never thought to ask anyone for a lift. 'She didn't recognise anyone else to talk to, but she talked to me.'

Len caught the Indian Pacific from Perth to Sydney when he was ninety-nine, carrying his old Globite case, secured with a leather belt. The tiny figure standing on the platform at Central Station looked, at one and the same time, vulnerable and indestructible. He marvelled at the number of women in Sydney who wore trousers and said he would fly to Sydney on his next visit.

Fred Kelly

1897–1998

1st Battalion Reinforcements

Frederick John Kelly's younger brother, Jim, dragged Fred into the army. It wasn't that Fred needed much dragging. He was eighteen, working as a clerk at Summer Hill and ready enough, but it was Jim who wanted most to go. Besides, Fred had a girlfriend, Nina Carless. 'Jim pestered the life out of mum,' Fred said. Bessie Kelly, born in Southampton, eventually gave permission for her two boys to enlist for king and empire.

The trouble was that Jim was only sixteen. Someone measured his chest and sent him away, too young and too skinny. Fred went for his medical and passed. Jim took the medical certificate from his brother and suggested that Fred could pass for himself again the next day. Fred agreed. The brothers both joined reinforcements for the 1st Battalion although, strictly speaking, Jim Kelly was not in the army. 'We pulled a swifty,' said Fred. The third Kelly brother, Mick, also tried to enlist. Their father, John, drew the line there and ordered Mick to withdraw his application. The boy, after all, was only fourteen.

Fred and Jim left Sydney in August 1915, on the cargo liner *Runic*, bound for Egypt. Fred recalled that the trip had much of the atmosphere of a holiday, the highlight being when the crew caught a shark from which Jim souvenired a tooth. Fred trained as a

gunner but succumbed to dysentery before his unit left for Gallipoli. He didn't reach the peninsula until October, by which time he discovered that the worst of the action at Gallipoli was over and Jim hadn't made it at all, having been sent home from Egypt with enteric fever.

'Gallipoli, as far as I was concerned, was a picnic,' said Fred, in a burst of unaccustomed hyperbole to illustrate the difference between the first months and the last. He spent two months in three-metre-deep trenches, with firing bays dug halfway up the trench wall. Despite the picnic, he was glad to get out of the frying pan. He couldn't have known he was headed for the fire itself.

Fred Kelly joined the Somme offensive with the 53rd Battalion of the 5th Division. He was the main gunner with a machine gun team and took part in the ill-planned diversion at Fromelles, where 5,533 men of the 5th Division were casualties in twenty-seven hours of destruction. Fromelles, in July 1916, was a bitter introduction for Australians to the savagery of the Western Front.

Fred returned to Grantham, Lincolnshire, in 1917 to train machine gunners. In 1918, he volunteered to rejoin his detachment on the Somme, a decision he described later as the worst of his life. He fought with the Australians who recaptured Villers-Bretonneux, an action critical to the course of the war and described later by General Sir John Monash: 'In my opinion, this counter-attack at night, without artillery support, is the finest thing yet done in the war by Australians or any other troops.'

Kelly was hit three times but not seriously wounded. He recalled being relieved on one occasion, returning behind the lines with shells exploding all around him and vomiting as he walked, weighed down by the machine gun. He carried a wallet in his breast pocket edged with a silver strip. The strip remained blackened forever, a reminder of Fred Kelly's hell on earth.

He came home promising never to fly, having seen war planes fall out of the sky, and never to leave Australia again. He kept both promises. Jim recovered from his fever and died of heart failure, aged sixty-two. Mick, having missed out on World War I, represented the family in World War II, was captured at Singapore, jailed at Changi and died of heart failure at fifty-six. Fred found that Nina had a new boyfriend, but she preferred her soldier. They married in 1919 and had seven children, including two boys. They lost their home in the Depression but Fred worked thirty-eight years with Nestlé, ultimately as company accountant.

Their elder son, John Kelly, went to World War II against his parents' wishes. 'I broke up the day he went,' Fred said. 'So did Nina. John said, "I'll be back", and out of my mouth came the words, "I don't think so".' John was killed by the Japanese in New Guinea.

Nina died in 1971. In 1996, Fred lived with a heart pacemaker, a bitser dog called Scruffy and two unmarried daughters, Doris and Daphne, who had been a missionary in Japan. Fred, who had been raised a Catholic, by this time called himself a rogue. He had never joined an ex-servicemen's association or attended an Anzac Day march.

Roy Kyle

1897–1996

24th Battalion

Albert Roy Kyle was a junior clerical officer in a bank when he enlisted at seventeen. He had grown up in the countryside around Corowa on the NSW–Victorian border, living 'the life of Huckleberry Finn', and had left school only fifteen months before joining the army. The wave of patriotism that swept Australia and 'romantic notions of military life' encouraged him to join, with enlistment pushed by posters, newspapers and women distributing white feathers to those who didn't sign up. 'The country was mad with patriotism. I couldn't get there quickly enough to kill a German.' His parents, similarly affected, saw little point in objecting to their son's intentions.

Roy's introduction to army life was not so romantic. He was stationed at Seymour, up to his neck in mud drills and training. He made friends with a young socialite from Sydney. 'He arrived with a trunk of fine clothes,' said Roy, 'monogrammed silk underwear and the like. The trunk was put outside the tent the first night and, by morning, all the underwear and other clothing was gone. A really nice fellow.'

His romantic notions of military life were reinforced by English and Scottish soldiers he saw in the Middle East, splendid in their military regalia, colourful tunics, kilts and bagpipes. Gallipoli, where he had his 18th birthday, revealed the reality of war. He went straight to Lone Pine and stayed there until

being one of the last evacuated in December. 'I volunteered to stay behind, patrolling up and down, firing the odd shot here and there. The most successful part of the campaign was the evacuation. But Gallipoli was a vile place. It was pretty ghastly. The Turks saw to that. It was bare and barren and we never held more than four hundred acres.'

He served in Egypt, then as a mortar operator in the trenches of France. He lost an older brother, Leonard, in France and brother-in-law at Passchendaele. An exploding howitzer shell ended his own war. 'Shells came down and almost landed on my head,' he recalled. 'One exploded over my head. I heard it coming, getting closer and closer and thought it was going to hit me in the chest.' Roy was wounded in the head, arms and back. He carried shrapnel in his back from then on. France, he said, was fiercer, wilder and deadlier than Gallipoli.

The armistice was signed while Roy was at sea on his way home. He disembarked in Adelaide and travelled to Melbourne by train. Women with cream cakes and other rich food greeted the walking wounded at every station. The food made him sick. Roy's mother, sister and aunts welcomed him in Melbourne, but he wasn't a hero to everyone. Melbourne 'louts' abused him because of his uniform. It took him six months to recuperate and he didn't want to return to the bank, but work was scarce and his employers had kept his job open. He was to stay with the bank for forty-four years, in New South Wales, Victoria and South Australia.

His family suffered again in World War II. Roy's sister Marjorie was returning from England when the ship on which she sailed was torpedoed off Jamaica. 'She was a lovely woman,' he said.

Roy reflected in retirement: 'Gallipoli woke Australia up a good deal. Before then we did what we were told. We were basically a colony, part of the British Empire. We always thought one Briton would beat ten Germans. The feeling of nationhood began with Gallipoli. But I don't take any pride in the medals at all. I was a silly boy and should have had my bottom smacked for joining up at that age.'

He met Jessie Johannsen at church and they married in 1920. Roy and Jessie were still holding hands and calling each other 'darling' in 1993, the year she died after seventy-three and a half years of marriage. 'I wouldn't part with a day of it,' Roy said. 'I have been very lonely without her. However, these things happen.' The couple had two children, five grandchildren and thirteen great-grandchildren. A photograph of Jessie had pride of place in Roy's retirement home room, showing a handsome woman with a strong face and smile, wearing a hat and a fur fashionable at the time.

He said in 1995: 'I used to say jokingly I would march on Anzac Day when I am the last Anzac left alive. Goodness me, I'm not far off it.'

A Turk had asked him in 1990: 'Why did you try to invade our country?'

Roy: 'We were part of the British Empire.'

Turk: 'We had an empire once.'

Roy Kyle was stopped by the short conversation. He saw an essential truth in it. Empires come and go. Enemies become friends, friends enemies. Everything changes. Little lasts.

Roy Longmore
1894–2001
21st Battalion

Young Roy Longmore was a bit of a devil. With his younger brothers, Hec and Charley, he once took a box of white mice to church and let them loose in the middle of the vicar's sermon. On other occasions the Longmore boys uncoupled the horses from their carriages outside church, throwing the elderly women drivers into disarray at the end of Sunday service.

Roy left school to work on his family's mixed farm at Bannockburn — a few cows, horses and apple orchards. Life in the countryside served him well for what lay ahead. The Longmores were a tough and self-sufficient lot. Roy was a crack shot, providing a steady supply of rabbits for the family table and friends.

When war broke out, he enlisted at Geelong Town Hall. He arrived at Gallipoli in August, with the 21st Battalion, 2nd Division. 'It was a nice picnic ground,' he recalled, in that laconic manner common to men of his time and his country. He said of the Turkish soldiers: 'They were pretty decent fighters, fair fighters, good soldiers.'

Roy never talked much about the war, another quality shared by men of his time. He never talked to his wife, nor their son, about it. It was only in the last six of his 107 years that he opened up a little. Even then he did not enjoy the talk. 'I'd sooner let bygones be bygones. What do you want to wake the whole thing up for? I don't want to go through it all again. They're no good, these wars. A lot of lives lost, no use at all. There's got to be another way of fixing up these rows without killing each other.'

He had gone away as an infantryman and arrived at Gallipoli as a sapper or digger, with the hazardous task of tunnelling through the hills of Gallipoli, placing mines under enemy trenches. 'I was underground most of the time. I didn't see much.' Perhaps it was a good thing he didn't see much or perhaps he saw more than he let on and that was the reason he never talked much. In any case, he was at Lone Pine, about which Private Richard Smith wrote in a letter home: 'We couldn't do anything about the dead. To bury them would be to join them.'

He didn't see himself as a hero, either. 'I don't know about that,' Roy said. 'We were just doing a job. The part that worried me most was when too many people got on the boat at the evacuation and we were stuck on a sandbar. We were sitting ducks, but we got out.'

Longmore 'boxed on' in Egypt and on the Somme, at those places where war reached its most awful — Pozières, Armentières, Villers-Bretonneux — before being badly wounded by machine gun fire a month before the war ended. It was the third time he had been wounded in action, and the last. He was to carry forever a deep indentation in his left leg, between knee and hip. 'I can't remember where I was bowled over,' he said, struggling with fading memory. 'Can't think of it these days. I was being treated in a hospital in England and one doctor was going to take my leg off at the hip but another doctor chap saved it. Marvellous. I was thinking of entering this year's Stawell Gift.'

Roy returned to Australia in 1919, medically unfit for an army that had seen enough killing and maiming and maddening, had no further need or appetite for it and was exhausted by it. When he limped through the front gate of his home, his father said: 'Glad to see you. Sit down and have a yarn.' He returned to the farm in 1920 but the war hadn't finished with him. His wounds made farming life too difficult. He opened a service station and car hire business in Malvern with brother Hec.

He married Lillian Taylor in 1927 and retired from full-time work in the 1950s to nurse his ailing wife. Their only child, Eric, had two sons and four granddaughters. Lillian Longmore died in 1979, when Roy went back to work, as a renovator. The war had changed him forever. Eric said he remained a fairly jovial chap but was much quieter. Much of the fun had gone out of his life, although he won many trophies for claybird shooting with the Blackburn Gun Club. He had long lost any urge to shoot at anything living. He moved later to a retirement home, keeping himself neat and sometimes watching television, his fading eyes a metre from the set. He was hunched over a little by then … 'I was quite a tall chap … six foot one inch …'

France awarded him the Legion of Honour in 1998 and he received the Australian Government's 80th Anniversary Armistice Remembrance Medal in 1999. In 2000, he featured with Alec Campbell and Walter Parker in Australia Post's stamp series, The Last Anzacs. He enjoyed meeting old comrades until they died, and ttook it upon himself to shepherd the blind Claude Fankhauser about Claude's house, offering a little advice: 'You must never race your heart. I never took exercise, was too lazy to play cricket and always went easy on my heart.'

At the end of the day, they would shake hands again at the front door.

Roy: 'See you again, old chap.'

Claude: 'Yes, you never know.'

Roy: 'I'll turn up like a bad penny.'

Claude: 'Ha ha. See you later. Ta ta.'

Ted Matthews
1896–1997
1st Division Signals

When Albert Edward Matthews arrived in Egypt on his way to Gallipoli, an Australian officer said: 'Ah, they're sending babies.' Ted was eighteen but looked younger. Heading towards his one hundredth birthday, on Armistice Day 1996, he still looked younger than his years. Yet he was the only Anzac still alive to have gone ashore on 25 April 1915, and he had stayed at Gallipoli longer than any other survivor.

Born in Leichhardt, Ted was one of six children. He was called Ted to distinguish him from his father, a paper bag merchant also named Albert. The young man was a carpenter when war broke out. He had been in the army cadets and knew how to handle a rifle but joined the 1st Division Signals because he knew morse code. He landed with the 1st Brigade on 25 April, to be greeted on the beach by a hunk of shrapnel in the chest. A thick notebook in his pocket saved his life.

Matthews didn't fire a shot at Gallipoli. 'The Signals had it easy compared to the infantry, who had a terrible time in the trenches. The AIF was the best infantry in the world. Mind you, we had to keep our heads down, too.' The closest he came to the action was when he was caught in the front line during an attack. Ted loaded rifles for his mates.

He turned nineteen at Gallipoli and was among the last evacuated on the night of 19 December and morning of 20 December. 'The idea of the invasion was good — if we had got through to Russia, it would have shortened the war. But they mucked it up. The planning was poor. Some people called us "five-bob-a-day murderers" but the politicians were the murderers. Politicians make up the wars. They don't go to them.'

He went on to fight in France and Belgium with

the 4th Division. 'They sent us to the hottest spots.' He rode a horse for three hours then marched for nineteen hours to get to Villers-Bretonneux. 'That victory helped end the war. It was good to be there. I went away a boy and came back a man. It was something that had to be done and I did it. Well, at least I helped.'

Back home, Ted returned to carpentry. He married Stella Brodrick and they had two girls. He found the Depression harder in many ways than the war. 'I only had myself to look after in the war. I had a family in the Depression.' Ted would walk twice a week from his home in Belmore to Circular Quay to register for work, to Railway Square to pick up food parcels, and back home, a distance of more than twenty kilometres. He set up a travelling library, packing books into a motorcycle sidecar, and later an old car, and driving them round the Sydney suburbs for a penny a book. He also made soft drinks.

He tried to enlist for World War II but was rejected because of his age. 'I'm glad I didn't have sons. They might have got messed up in the second war.' His daughters, Jean and Irene, both married American servicemen. 'The silly girls thought American men superior to Australians.' After Stella died, Ted married her best friend, Freda Corlett. After Freda's death, Ted went to live in Florida with Irene but returned to Australia after seventeen years so as not to be a burden to his daughters and to be 'with my own people, my own kind'. He had nine grandchildren in the United States, but moved into the war veterans' home at Narrabeen, where one wall in his room carried a faded print of George Lambert's painting of the Gallipoli landing, with the Australians clambering up the cliffs under fire. 'You know, I can't remember climbing up there.'

Although a little unsteady on his feet, he walked without a stick. He said: 'If I could get some new legs, I'd be all right. I haven't had time to die yet. Irene's husband went for a cup of coffee and dropped dead. That's how I would like to go, without the coffee.'

When visitors thanked him for his good cheer and his time he would say: 'I've all the time in the world. Time is all I have left.' He died peacefully in his sleep.

The people of Australia made Ted Matthews grander in death than he had ever claimed to be in life. The Governor-General, Sir William Deane, called him 'the quintessential Australian' and said that the national significance of his loss was 'about the spirit, the depth, the meaning, the very essence of our nation'. The Prime Minister, John Howard, said that 9 December, the day Ted Matthews died, should be marked 'as the day Australia grew old enough to sometimes forget what happened that Anzac Day [1915] but determined enough to always remember'. He added: 'To those of us who lead nations, let us recall that it was Matthews who said, "Politicians make up the wars. They don't go to them".'

When the old soldier's casket left St Stephen's Uniting Church in Macquarie Street, Joy Foster, of Newcastle, waved a large Australian flag and called out 'cooee', the rallying call for World War I. Carol Lane, of St Peters, began clapping and the clapping spread through the waiting crowd, lifting the solemnity of the moment. 'It's a bonzer day for a bonzer bloke,' she said in the language of yesteryear. At the service at Northern Suburbs Crematorium, just before a stone and sand from Gallipoli beach were scattered on the coffin, and before his mother hushed him, Adoniram Matthews began to sing Happy Birthday. He was not yet two years old and scarcely knew Grand-Uncle Ted, but the nation will ensure that the boy gets to know the man.

Harry Newhouse
1895–1996
4th Battalion

Born in Pyrmont, Harry left school at fourteen and volunteered in October 1914, 'for king and country'. His father had recently died and his brother, George, was already in the AIF. Presenting himself at Victoria Barracks he was told that as a railwayman he should stay to look after the railways. 'Well, you protect them while I'm away,' he said.

George Newhouse landed under fire at Anzac Cove on 25 April 1915, and Harry, with the 4th Battalion and under fire, on 26 April. Harry learned a few days later that George had died at Shrapnel Gully. 'Poor old George. I would have been with George if I could.'

Eighty years later, he still lamented George and pondered occasionally on the meaning of it all: 'Not only did my brother get killed and a lot of our men, but there were 86,000 Turks killed. The Turks never did anything to us and we never did anything to the Turks.

We did not think we were going to fight them, poor buggers. We were going to fight the Germans. I'm only here because I could sidestep better than George. What was it for? I don't know. It should never have been. But you have to take your cap off to the Turks.'

He remembered the stink of corpses, millions of flies, dysentery, hunger and thirst. He told of the day at Anzac Cove when he went for rations. When he returned both his dugout and all his mates had been blown up. He was dug in on Shrapnel Gully when a Turkish bullet hit his food tin and ricocheted into his forehead. 'Down I went like a log. They bound up my forehead so I looked like the Rajah of Poonacoota but soon I was stricken with pneumonia and pleurisy and the stretcher-bearers had to carry me down to the field ambulance on the beach. I felt sorry for those blokes under fire just for me.'

Harry recovered at a military hospital near Alexandria and was on his way back to Gallipoli when struck down with malaria. He was sent to hospital in Lemnos and then home. 'I wasn't a real hero. I don't know what to think I was. I think I was a bit of a nincompoop.' He said of World War I in general: 'They think we became a nation, but they killed half the nation.'

He returned to the railways as a maintenace worker, married Eliza Green in 1917 and they lived at Kirribilli. Harry and Eliza — he always called her Lila — celebrated the end of the war in 1918 with their baby boy. They named their son after his brother, George. Harry fought at Sydney Stadium as a welterweight — 'I didn't lose all the time' — and occasionally in the local pub. He became a champion bridge player with the Railways Institute. He taught young George and Harry's daughter, Nola, how to fish. Young George recalled his father reminiscing on Anzac Days about seventy years ago: 'I was there, son. I lost my mate, my brother, there.' In 1996, Harry was still calling his son 'Young George'. Young George, then seventy-eight, said his father had also taught them about respect for elders and for essential decency.

After Harry's retirement in 1958, the Newhouses built a house at Saratoga, on the NSW central coast. Eliza died in 1968 but he had seven great-grandchildren and a great-great-grandchild. He went back to Gallipoli in 1990 with his 4th Battalion mate Jack Ryan, saw where brother George had fallen in Shrapnel Gully and discovered his brother's name on the Lone Pine memorial. Jack Ryan, who also went ashore on 25 April, was wounded at Lone Pine and twice wounded in France.

In 1996, Young George was still visiting his father every Friday at the nursing home, where they shared three cans of beer and worked out their bets on the horses for the next day. Harry was concerned about the disqualification of jockey Jim Cassidy for three years. He had often backed Cassidy's mounts. 'I don't suppose I'll be backing him any more.'

By then, Harry Newhouse was living from one anniversary to the next, eating porridge, toast and tea for breakfast, a beer and a banana for lunch. Young George, who remembered the old man's strength, saw the muscle fall from his body. His hearing had never been the same after the pounding of the guns at Gallipoli. Yet the old man never complained. When another old man in the retirement home took leave of his senses and hit Harry Newhouse with a walking stick, the old Anzac was simply puzzled. 'You know, son, he wouldn't have done that to me a couple of years ago.'

Harry led the 1995 Anzac Day march in Gosford, in a vintage car. Then he hung on for his one hundredth birthday in September, with a party at Gosford RSL and a telegram from the Queen. 'Not many people live to one hundred,' he said with satisfaction. Then he looked forward to the 1995 Melbourne Cup, tipping Doriemus to nursing staff at his retirement home and backing it himself. It won, paying $9.90 for a $1 bet. Harry Newhouse did not gloat about his triumph; that was never his way. He just smiled the big smile that lit up a good few lives and set himself for 1996 and, perhaps, the next Melbourne Cup. He died a few weeks after the 1996 Cup. Saintly won the race, at 8:1. Harry Newhouse deserved to have backed it.

Walter Parker
1894–2000
20th Battalion

An apprentice commercial art printer in Sydney, Walter Parker joined up to serve the king. His father signed his papers on condition he not serve in New Guinea because of the threat of malaria. Young Wal thought he was going to fight in England. He was to find greater threats elsewhere.

Wal was born in Brookvale, the youngest of eight children, including five girls. His father owned a lot of land in the Manly area, in the days when much of the district was divided into self-sufficient farmlets and Chinese gardens. Parker senior brought his family up to be God-fearing and God-loving. He was wealthy enough to give a block of land to the Anglican Church and another for the building of a school.

Wal's best mate at school in Brookvale was Norm Craven. The two young men enlisted on the same day, although they didn't know this until they landed in the same tent in camp. They landed at Gallipoli together, too, as reinforcements for the 20th Battalion. The worst of the fighting had passed. 'I'm glad he went later rather than earlier,' said Gwen Charlesworth, his daughter, 'or he might not be my father.'

His first job was to carry water and ammunition to the 'scary lot' of men in the front line. 'They looked awful but they were a grateful lot of chaps.' Pipes of frozen water were uncoupled and carried to the front line, to provide the men with water when the ice melted. His hardest task was to write letters home,

Walter Parker with daughter Gwen Charlesworth.

letters that were 'not too hard' but let loved ones know that it was not 'all love and honey'.

Having survived Gallipoli, Wal and Norm went to France together, to Pozières and the Somme. Shrapnel cut a tendon in Wal's left arm, a disability he carried for the rest of his life. He recovered in hospital but the wound ended Wal's war. Wal found Norm again in hospital, in the next bed. His mate had been wounded, too, but not seriously. 'There are so many Manly boys over here,' said Norm, 'you wonder whether any are left at home.' While Wal went home, Norm returned to the front, was blown up and suffered massive stomach wounds from which he was lucky to recover.

Back home, Walter missed the mateship that had surrounded him at war. After four years living outdoors, even in the mud, he didn't fancy life as a printer. He and Norm headed north to Mullumbimby, on the NSW north coast, working on dairy and banana farms, and marrying Mullumbimby girls. When disease ruined their bananas, Norm headed back to Sydney while Wal went to Glen Innes with the woman he had married in 1920, Amy McPhail. He grew vegetables and worked in a store; she grew flowers.

Their only son, Earle, was a rear-gunner in Lancaster bombers when shot down and killed over Germany in World War II. Tall and good-looking, he had not turned twenty-one. The family had sent presents and a birthday cake. 'We made a good foursome,' Gwen Charlesworth said. 'We shared everything together. We all missed him.' Earle did not leave home until February 1943, but he was dead by October that year. Mrs Charlesworth kept his letters. The last one said how much he had enjoyed the tin of peaches the family had sent. Wal had tried to join the home construction corps set up by Prime Minister John Curtin but was rejected because of his World War I injury.

He used to be the life of family parties. During their fifty-two years of marriage before Amy died, she would say: 'Wal, do you really need to laugh that loud?' Twenty-four years after her death, blind and in failing health, he said: 'I still miss her, but that's life and death.'

He believed his God guided lives during war and still guided the survivors. For a long period after losing his sight with glaucoma he would listen to hymns on tape. He never made anything of his blindness. Quite suddenly one day in 1996, he broke from a reverie after a meal, in prayer: 'Dear God, I just want to thank you for the food, for the lovely day and for the people here. I think that's all I can say now.'

'I did worry I was losing him,' his daughter said. 'But I have come to terms with it. He is over 100 and he has been a good father. There have been no momentous occasions in our lives. They have been comfortable, happy and home-making, like the lives of so many Australians.' He died peacefully, just a day after Australia Post issued the set of stamps bearing his photograph — and those of Alec Campbell and Roy Longmore — as young soldiers.

Bob Ponsford

1894–1996

24th Battalion

Robert Leslie Ponsford was the youngest of eight children, two sisters who became nurses and six brothers who went to war. Eldest brother Frank joined first, as a doctor in the British Army. Claude was a dentist in the AIF, Ralph a farmer who enlisted in the AIF, Walter an optician in the AIF, Leonard and Bob, both in the AIF. Bob said the enlistments were hard on his parents, Walter and Thirza, particularly his mother.

He had been dux of Hawthorn College, Melbourne, in Year 11 and went to Scotch College for the last year of his school education. He didn't like returning to the school afterwards because he was reminded of all the friends killed in war. Of fifty members of the Kooyong lacrosse teams with whom he'd played, forty-eight joined up.

Bob's first attempt to enlist was rejected on the grounds of poor eyesight, but the chief medical officer overturned this ruling on the basis that the Ponsfords were great sea captains in the days of Sir Francis Drake. When young Ponsford's records were lost he had to reapply and was rejected again because of his eyesight. Nonetheless, he joined the 24th Battalion. 'A bit of skulduggery went on,' he said. In fact, a lieutenant forged the doctor's signature.

Bob trained in Egypt, visited the pyramids and the Sphinx and later recalled Australians making their presence felt by overturning fruit barrows in the streets of Cairo. He landed at Anzac Cove on the night of 5 September, jumping into the water with rifle, ammunition and a heavy pack containing three

days' rations — 2.5 kg of bully beef and dry biscuits for lunch. The men of the 24th were marched up the nearest steep hill, marched back down for lunch and sent up again.

He recalled Lone Pine as 'one of the hottest spots': 'There had been terrible fighting there and many killed on both sides. The trenches were so mingled up. We were just told, 'here's the trench and there's the Turkish trench'. I fired a few shots off and, to my horror, saw an Australian hat where I'd been firing. Some bloke had been shooting at us. The whole thing was confusing. We'd build up our trench with sandbags in the night-time and the Turks would blow it down in the daytime and this went on day after day, night after night.'

He celebrated his twenty-first birthday in the trenches, eating a chocolate cake and a tin of pineapple sent by brother Wally from Alexandria. He was among the last out in December, sailing away on a British battleship with tubs of hot water along the deck for the men who had not bathed properly for months.

Ponsford went to Egypt, where he was 'claimed' by his dentist brother Claude to work as an army dental assistant. The brothers moved from one town to the next around the French–Belgian border, performing dental work in improvised surgeries just behind the British and Australian lines. The experience with the 2nd Field Ambulance brought him his most vivid memory of the war: 'Icicles hung from the barbed-wire fence … about nine inches long. It was very tough.'

He rode a bicycle to Ypres, in Belgium, looking for his brother, Len. As he rode he heard the sound of bullets whizzing overhead and of gunfire. On arrival he discovered he had ridden between the lines in no-man's-land, with a German guard post overlooking the route. Len vanished in the bloody bombardment of Pozières. He was never seen again and no one knows exactly what happened to him.

Back home, Bob rejoined the AMP, where he worked for forty-six years, becoming assistant manager in Victoria. When he was sixty, the company offered him three years' pension as a lump sum. Ponsford declined with thanks, choosing to continue with his company pension. 'I intend living for a good while yet,' he said. In 1996 he had been retired for thirty-eight years.

His marriage to Jean Mortimer lasted even longer, fifty-eight years until her death in 1982. They had a son, three grandchildren and nephews and nieces all over the place. The Ponsfords built a house in Camberwell and the old Anzac still lived there in 1996, though his eyesight had 'gone a bit' and his hearing had 'gone a bit'. He scorned any suggestion that he move into a nursing home because they were 'full of old people'. Eighty-one years after Gallipoli, Bob Ponsford still valued the experience. As a hero? 'Oh no!'

James Sinton
1894–1995
Otago Mounted Rifles

One of James Sinton's clearest memories of Gallipoli was sitting next to a mate, eating bully beef, when a Turkish sniper's bullet caught his friend right between the eyes. He died the next day. Another memory was of his 'playing possum' in a field of dead and wounded, as Turkish soldiers went round bayoneting the enemy, making sure the wounded joined their dead comrades. Trooper Sinton, of the Otago Mounted Rifles, New Zealand Expeditionary Force, kept very still indeed. He lived to tell the tale to his seven sons, all of whom fought in World War II or Korea. William Sinton, James's elder brother, also served at Gallipoli, winning the Military Medal, and another brother, Albert, served in France. The Sinton family's readiness to answer their country's call might have established a record for a family in international conflict.

James Sinton, or Jimmy, as he was generally known, died in the last days of 1995. He had suffered several strokes and could not speak for some time before his death. Records of his service were sketchy. However, his son Alex kept his father's service medal — 'Trooper James Sinton 9/966 NZEF'. Alex, who wore the medal around his neck during World War II, told how his father's first attempt at enlistment had been refused, perhaps because of his age.

Jimmy Sinton was born in Tiniroto, New Zealand, to parents from Scotland. He began work at fourteen on sheep stations. After being turned down for war service, he and a mate promptly jumped on a ship at Wairoa, sailed to Dunedin and joined the Otago Mounted Rifles. He went to Egypt and recalled wading ashore at Gallipoli, his rifle above his head.

'The Turks were up there and we were down here,' he said. 'They were cutting us down.'

He recalled the stench of decaying bodies and the armistice on 24 May, when the Turks and Allied troops put down their weapons and brandished shovels to bury their dead in no-man's-land, chatting and exchanging cigarettes on one of the most poignant days in the history of warfare and one which is touched with surrealism around the turn of the 20th century.

He recalled, too, the evacuation of Gallipoli, which some observers called the most successful part of the whole sorry affair. The Allies escaped without loss. Trooper Sinton remembered the elaborate evacuation plans, including erection of a device which enabled water to drip from one can to another, thereby depressing triggers on rifles which fired off odd, ghostly shots designed to convince the Turks that the enemy was still on their peninsula. 'If anyone makes a sound,' Jimmy Sinton's sergeant warned, 'I'll blow his bloody head off!'

After evacuation, he used his cavalry skills in Palestine, with the 5th Australian Light Horse, and he went to France, where he saw the muddy, bloody horror of Passchendaele and the Somme.

Back in New Zealand, Sinton mustered cattle, managed farming properties and married Rebecca Ryan in 1921. 'He was a workaholic,' said son Ivor. 'He was tough but fair,' said son Alex. He was tough all right. He took over the family farm in Tiniroto at the end of the 1920s, at the onset of the Depression. With wool down to about a penny a pound the Depression crippled his family. The 1931 earthquake badly damaged the homestead, which finally burnt down in 1932. Sinton lost all his wool but the succession of disasters could not break him. He went droving, known as 'the gentleman drover' because he always wore a tie. Then he turned to managing properties.

He suffered his first stroke around 1960. Later he broke his neck when a horse fell on him. Rebecca died in 1981. He celebrated his one hundredth birthday in a nursing home in Taradale, near Napier, after moving there from Te Awamutu to be closer to two sons. Nurses remember how he didn't want to cut his cake. Jimmy Sinton was embarrassed by the fuss.

Bert Smith
1896–1996
1st Division Signals

War hurried in on young William Herbert Smith. Herbert, as his family called him, or Bert, the name his wife preferred, recalled the Australia of 1914 as a peaceful place. The young man had a job with the Commonwealth Bank in Melbourne, secured by his father with payment of a small lump sum, which sounds like a bribe today but was regarded as a bond then. The country was untroubled by the tensions building in Europe. The future for the nation, and for a young man with a job in the bank, was bright.

The murder of Archduke Franz Ferdinand of Austria–Hungary in Sarajevo on 28 June 1914 changed all that. With the declaration of war, Australia pledged support to Britain and there was an immediate rush to enlist. Bert enlisted at eighteen. 'It

seemed the obvious thing to do. The love of adventure and the natural affinity with England played a part. In 1914 most Australians were of British stock. All my friends were joining up and I wasn't going to be left behind.' Bert Smith's grandparents were English. Even his mother expected him to enlist. 'Yes, I suppose you must,' she said.

He joined the Signals School, hoping it would be more interesting than infantry training. Posted to 1st Division Signals, he contracted measles in camp in Victoria. He broke out of camp and went home rather than be told he could not go to Gallipoli. When he returned to camp five days later, without spots, his absence had gone unnoticed. On the troopship bound for Gallipoli from Lemnos, 'we were a bit excited but

tried not to show it. I remember a few of us filling in the time with a game of cards, trying to look as if this sort of thing happened every day.'

Communication at Gallipoli was by telephone. When the wire was cut, the signaller would dash out to mend it. Bert carried a British brigadier's periscope in Shrapnel Gully. He recalled the living conditions: 'Worst of all was the great shortage of water. Each man was allowed only one pannikin per week. This had to serve all purposes! The staple diet consisted of bully beef and rock-hard biscuits which had to be soaked in one's tea to be edible at all.' He caught the mumps at Gallipoli, spending two weeks in a makeshift hospital on the beach. He recalled the evacuation with greater pleasure: 'It was a bitterly cold night and we had to wait on the beach for about eight hours. But we arrived safely at Lemnos the next morning and that was the end of Gallipoli for us.'

His elder brother, Percy, fought in France with the 4th Division Signals and, on one occasion, the brothers exchanged dugouts. At the Somme in 1916 Bert Smith took part in the recapture of Pozières. Expecting the German bombardment to be so intense that telephone communications would be impossible, Bert was one of three signallers who maintained a visual signalling station on higher ground overlooking the frontline battalions. The Germans saw his morse flag and made him a target. 'I was fortunate to get out in one piece.'

Smith was conscious throughout the war that his education had been cut short and he would have to make up the leeway. Back home, he studied accountancy, joined the Taxation Department, and specialised in the study of case law, appearing as an advocate for the Taxation Commissioner before the old Board of Review. Among other tasks in Canberra, he wrote a detailed second reading speech for one of Treasurer Ben Chifley's Taxation Bills.

He had met Alice Barnett at the guest house she ran in Healesville with her two sisters. Bert booked in for a week, stayed a month and finally married Alice in 1925. They had a son, Alan Kaye-Smith, four grandchildren and, by 2002, five great-grandchildren. Alice died in 1963. 'I wouldn't recommend being alone to anyone, but you have to get used to it,' Bert said.

He worked until he was seventy-nine. He played the organ and was still reading the newspaper and large-print books in 1996, completing crosswords and playing the occasional game of scrabble and chess. 'Hero? No, one doesn't think of oneself as a hero, although I suppose April 25 1915 made a lasting impression on the nation. There are none of my crowd left.'

Bert Smith standing (right) in 1915.

Cedric Stapylton-Smith

1891–1996

New Zealand 5th Reinforcements

Cedric Drysdale Stapylton-Smith apologised for his name. 'Cousins in England weren't satisfied with the Smith so added the Stapylton, with a 'y' instead of an 'e', and the hyphen. Bloody nuisance.' War, too, was a bloody nuisance, although Cedric never entertained doubts about going. 'It was up to us all.' A woolclasser, he returned to New Zealand from working in Australia, paid off his debts — that was important to him — and enlisted with the 5th Reinforcements, Canterbury Regiment. 'I wasn't excited. I wasn't worried. I hadn't the foggiest idea what was in front of me.'

He went via Egypt to Gallipoli, landing in the middle of the awful battles of August. General Sir Ian Hamilton had planned an advance by the Anzac forces up the ridges to the commanding heights of the Sari Bair range, with a feint at Lone Pine and an attack at Suvla Bay. The Australian Light Horse made their notoriously ill-fated charge across the Nek. Historian C.E.W. Bean wrote of Lone Pine: 'The dead lay so thick that the only respect which could be paid to them was to avoid treading on their faces.'

'Gallipoli was a disaster,' Cedric said. 'It's marvellous that we did as well as we did. We didn't

have a hope of beating the Turks. We underestimated Johnny Turk, and Kemal Atatürk was a splendid officer, as game as they make them. We had respect for the Turks. They were clean fighters. Kitchener had no idea of what we were up against. Mind you, when things go wrong, we always blame the heads, the officers. I lost a lot of friends.'

Cedric was evacuated with dysentery, recovered and was sent back, finally being in the last group to leave in December. He went, via Egypt, from the frying pan of Gallipoli into the fire of Armentières and the Somme. 'The British guns sounded "bang-whizz" from behind, while the German guns replied "whizz-bang" from in front. The German guns were so good they could hit a clothes line.' He survived the Somme only to be wounded in a 'quiet sector' in April 1917, taking a short cut behind Allied lines to pick up the company's mail. A German shell smashed his left leg. 'Thank Christ,' I thought. 'Blighty at last.'

An English surgeon wanted to amputate his leg, but another doctor disagreed and won the argument. Cedric pushed his plastercast through a porthole on his homecoming ship into Auckland harbour and put a boot on his left foot for the first time in about a year. He had sailed away after paying his debts. He was to sail home with both boots on.

Stapylton-Smith went farming, like so many returned men, and married Grace Gardner in 1928. 'My wife thought a lot of me. I don't know whether she was much of a judge of character.' He studied singing and became well known as a baritone in the 1930s, 'singing anything from grand opera down'.

He drove a car until he was 103. 'The car was buggered. It gave up before me.' He was still reading newspapers in 1996 and taking at least a double whisky every day — three doubles on Wednesdays and Sundays, when the Rannerdale 'home of rest and relaxation' held social gatherings. And he was smoking seven or eight cigarettes a day. He had smoked since he was ten and his lungs remained clear, so he couldn't see much point in stopping.

'My whole life has been pretty fortunate,' he said, 'not a dog's life. A bloke in front of me in France was hit by a bullet which went right through him and just nicked me. I get sick of being asked the recipe for old age. I haven't gone without anything. My mother, Mary Euphemia, lived to be over ninety. But I don't know that you should live a day beyond a hundred. Then all sorts of little things start to go wrong.'

He said the Lord's Prayer every night and prayed for the young people, so their world would be less troubled than his. Occasionally, particularly when prompted by Jessie Keown, a nursing aid who played piano, Cedric Drysdale Stapylton-Smith showed off his rich baritone:

Because God made thee mine
I'll cherish thee …

He died peacefully in his sleep, half an hour after taking his customary scotch.

Cedric Stapylton-Smith (left).

Albert White

1895–1997
25th Battalion

Albert White had never been interviewed about his war and, eighty years after Gallipoli, was not about to change his mind. He agreed to be photographed, however, then changed his mind and changed it back again, exercising a right that goes with extreme age and famous deeds. His near-sightless eyes twinkled defiance, on the back porch of his old Queenslander home, where he had lived alone for fourteen years since his wife, Eileen, died. Here he did his own washing and some cooking. He walked to the shops. A daughter lived in Texas, having married an American during World War II, but a son lived nearby and visited regularly. 'You insult him if you try to do anything,' said Alan White.

Albert had come from England at seventeen but headed back north two years later with the 25th Battalion. Army records show he was admitted to hospital at Gallipoli and wounded by a bullet in an arm on the Somme in 1918. 'I'll say one thing,' he said at the top of his back steps before waving goodbye: 'Gallipoli was a bastard of a place.'

A few months later, Albert changed his mind again, encouraged by his family. He would try to remember, for the record. Born in London, he had come to Australia because his elder brother, Jim, wanted to come. Albert idolised Jim. He was torn between his mother and brother. His father, James White, said: 'If you want to go, go, but don't come

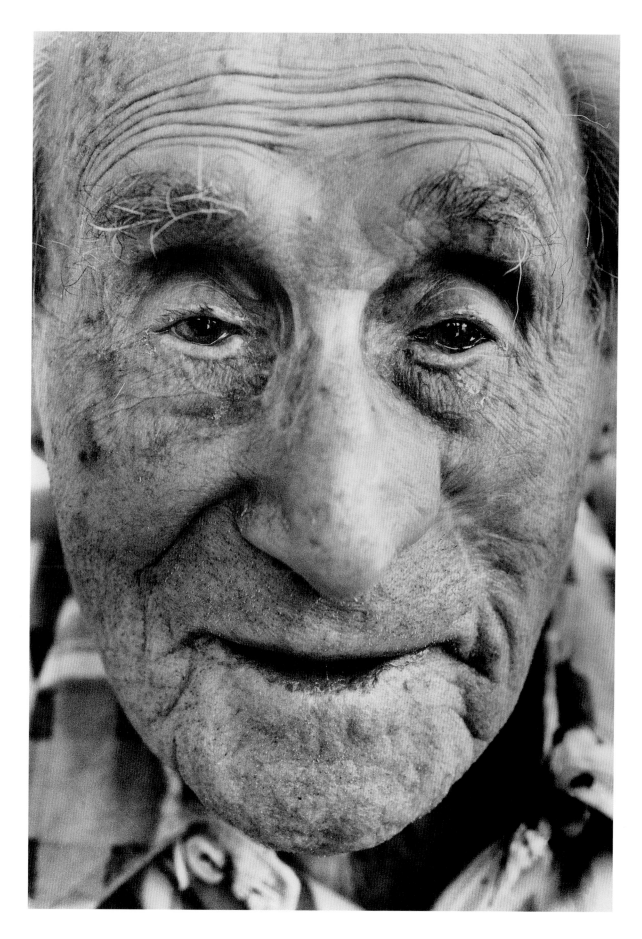

crying when it's time to go.' It was the one time Albert White saw tears in his father's eyes.

He thought Australia a 'bloody awful place' and wrote home saying he would be back to become a professional footballer. Jim intercepted the letter and gave Albert a dressing down. He stayed in Australia, to fight for the empire. 'I went because most of my cobbers went. Mates from my soccer team went, the goalkeeper went, not that I bloody wanted to go.'

What he remembered most about Gallipoli were the flies and the lice, crawling over his body. 'Don't mention flies to me. I hate the sight of them. You didn't have time to put jam on your bread. They would beat you to it.' He fought on Cheshire Ridge and up on The Apex. 'I never understood what we were fighting for,' he admitted cheerfully. 'It never crossed my mind. All I could think of was that I never wanted to go back to the bloody place.'

The Somme was worse. 'I enjoyed myself in Armentières. That was a great place, that Armentières. You could get out of the trenches on leave and go into town. Pozières wasn't much fun, though.' According to Bean's history, the 25th suffered more than any other battalion at Pozières, losing twenty-five officers and 660 other ranks. Albert was hit in the arm and caught on the edge of a bomb blast. 'We were blown up, all right. We went up like angels. I kept thinking I didn't want to lose my leg because I still wanted to become a professional footballer.'

Hospitalised in France, White was arrested for being on officer's premises and sent back to the line, where he developed scabies and trench foot. 'We were standing in mud up to our knees for a fortnight. Your feet can turn black.'

He sailed back to Australia after the Armistice, 'playing up in the Suez Canal' on the way. In Melbourne he found people wearing masks against the influenza epidemic that killed more people than did the war. In Moreton Bay, Albert and his comrades, itching to get home, were taken into quarantine for a week.

Eileen Campbell, who had been his girlfriend before he sailed for Gallipoli, tapped him on the shoulder when he walked down Queen Street, Brisbane, for the first time — and kissed him. 'I didn't like that, you know, in public.' They married in 1921 and were together for sixty years until her death.

Albert White spent most of the rest of his working life as a painter. He wouldn't attend Anzac Day parades. Yet his only real regret was that his eyesight was too poor for him to be able to study the race form. He shopped alone at Toombul in suburban Brisbane, waiting for the buzzer at traffic lights to cross the road, ignoring the escalator to take steps up and over the street. 'That's my exercise.' He gardened. 'Geraniums make a good show. They don't need much water … a few rose bushes. I dig a lot of things up that shouldn't be dug up.'

He had given up smoking — 'If you didn't have cigarettes on Gallipoli, you'd go fucking mad' — and was thinking of buying a mouth organ. He tapped his feet and hummed along to old songs played on the radio. 'What I do today is forgotten tomorrow. That's how my whole life has been, really.'

Colonel

He rode a white horse
heading the Anzac Day parade
fought at Ladysmith
and Gallipoli
was 90
tall
and treated me as his batman

helping him
down the hospital corridor
seemed holding rare archaeology
by the elbow

I apologised for clumsiness
he said 'never mind Sister
every beginning is difficult'
but he said it in Latin

his marriage of 60 years ended
when she died
he ran the funeral elegantly
with military style
and died a month later.

Kate Llewellyn

ANZAC Cove

There's a lonely stretch of hillocks:
There's a beach asleep and drear:
There's a battered broken fort beside the sea.
There are sunken trampled graves:
And a little rotting pier:
And winding paths that wind unceasingly.

There's a torn and silent valley:
There's a tiny rivulet
With some blood upon the stones beside its mouth.
There are lines of buried bones:
There's an unpaid waiting debt:
There's a sound of gentle sobbing in the South.

Leon Gellert,
January, 1916

THOSE HEROES THAT SHED THEIR BLOOD

AND LOST THEIR LIVES ...

YOU ARE NOW LYING IN THE SOIL OF A FRIENDLY COUNTRY

THEREFORE REST IN PEACE.

THERE IS NO DIFFERENCE BETWEEN THE JOHNNIES

AND THE MEHMETS TO US WHERE THEY LIE SIDE BY SIDE

HERE IN THIS COUNTRY OF OURS ...

YOU, THE MOTHERS,

WHO SENT THEIR SONS FROM FAR AWAY COUNTRIES

WIPE AWAY YOUR TEARS;

YOUR SONS ARE NOW LYING IN OUR BOSOM

AND ARE IN PEACE.

AFTER HAVING LOST THEIR LIVES ON THIS LAND THEY HAVE

BECOME OUR SONS AS WELL.

Atatürk, 1934
The inscription on the Turkish memorial to the Anzacs at Gallipoli

Bibliography

Adam-Smith, Patsy. *The Anzacs*, Nelson, Melbourne 1978.
Akcelik, Rahmi, ed. *Before and After Gallipoli*, Australian–Turkish Friendship Society Publications, Melbourne 1986.
Andrews, E.M., *The Anzac Illusion*, Cambridge University Press 1993.
Bean, C.E.W. *Gallipoli Mission*, Australian War Memorial, Canberra 1948.
Bean, C.E.W. *Official History of Australia in the War of 1914–1918*, Vols 1–6, Angus & Robertson, Sydney, 1921–42.
Bean, C.E.W., ed. *The Anzac Book*, Cassell, London 1916.
Boyack, Nicholas and Tolerton, Jane. *In the Shadow of War*, Penguin, Auckland 1990.
Churchill, W.S. *The World Crisis — The Eastern Front*, Thornton Butterworth, London 1931.
Clark, C.M.H. *A History of Australia*, Vol. 5, Melbourne University Press, Melbourne 1981.
Dennis, Peter et al, eds. *The Oxford Companion to Australian Military History*, Oxford University Press 1995.
Facey, Albert. *A Fortunate Life*, Fremantle Arts Centre Press, Fremantle 1981.
Fewster, Kevin and others. *A Turkish View of Gallipoli: Canakkale*, Hodja Educational Resources, Melbourne 1985.
Firkins, Peter. *The Australians in Nine Wars*, Hale, London 1972.
Gammage, Bill. *The Broken Years*, Penguin, Melbourne 1975.
Macdonald, Lyn. *1915: The Death of Innocence*, Headline, London 1993.
McKernan, Michael. *The Australian People and the Great War*, Nelson, Melbourne 1980.
Masefield, John. *Gallipoli*, Heinemann, London 1916.
Moorehead, Alan. *Gallipoli*, Hamilton, London 1956.
Robson, L.L. *The First AIF*, Melbourne University Press 1982.
Souter, Gavin. *Lion & Kangaroo*, Collins, Sydney 1976.
Souter, Gavin. *Mosman: a History*, Melbourne 1994.
Steel, Nigel and Hart, Peter. *Defeat at Gallipoli*, Macmillan, London 1994.
Thomson, Alistair. *Anzac Memories: Living with the Legend*, Oxford University Press 1994.
Tuchman, Barbara. *The Guns of August*, Constable, London 1962.
Tuchman, Barbara. *The March of Folly*, Alfred A. Knopf, New York 1984.

JOURNALS

Current Affairs Bulletin, April 1988
Journal of the Australian War Memorial, April 1983 and April 1991
The Lone Hand, October 1915
Sydney Morning Herald, 3 August 1914–29 May 1915, 25 April 1921, 26 April 1990

POETRY

'Anzac Cove' by Leon Gellert, *Songs of a Campaign*. Angus & Robertson (1917).
'Christ At Gallipoli' by Geoff Page, *Selected Poems*. Angus & Robertson (1991).
'Colonel' by Kate Llewellyn, *Trader Kate and the Elephants*. Friendly Street Poets (1982).
'On The Dead In Gallipoli' by John Masefield, *Selected Poems of John Masefield*. Heinemann (1978).
'Pioneer Lane' by Michael Dransfield, *Michael Dransfield Collected Poems*. University of Queensland Press (1987).
'1915' by Roger McDonald, *Airship*. University of Queensland Press (1975).

Biographies

Tony Stephens was born in Goulburn in 1939, three weeks after the outbreak of World War II, in which his father was killed by the Japanese. He writes for the *Sydney Morning Herald*.

Steven Siewert was born in Sydney in 1964, the son of a German father and Irish mother who came to Australia after World War II. He is a photographer with the *Sydney Morning Herald*.

Dr Michael McKernan is one of Australia's leading historians. He has held various senior positions at the Australian War Memorial since 1981.

This edition published 2003 by
FREMANTLE ARTS CENTRE PRESS
25 Quarry Street, Fremantle
(PO Box 158, North Fremantle 6159)
Western Australia.
www.facp.iinet.net.au

First published 1996 by Allen & Kelmsley Publishing, Mosman.

Copyright © Tony Stephens and Steven Siewert, 1996.

This book is copyright. Apart from any fair dealing for the purpose of private study, research,
criticism or review, as permitted under the Copyright Act, no part may be reproduced by any
process without written permission. Enquiries should be made to the publisher.

Designer Marion Duke.
Production Coordinator Cate Sutherland.
Printed by South Wind Productions, Singapore.

National Library of Australia
Cataloguing-in-publication data

Stephens, Tony.
The Last Anzacs.

Bibliography.
ISBN 1 92073 136 9.

1. Australia. Army. Australian and New Zealand Army Corps.
2. World War, 1914–1918 — Personal narratives, Australian.
3. World War, 1914-1918 — Campaigns — Turkey — Gallipoli Peninsula — Personal
narratives, Australian. 4. Veterans – Australia – Interviews. I. Title.

940.48194

The State of Western Australia has made an investment in this project through ArtsWA
in association with the Lotteries Commission.